GUNS
AND CRIME
THE DATA DON'T LIE

GUNS AND CRIME
THE DATA DON'T LIE

Mark Gius

CRC Press
Taylor & Francis Group
Boca Raton London New York

CRC Press is an imprint of the
Taylor & Francis Group, an **informa** business

CRC Press
Taylor & Francis Group
6000 Broken Sound Parkway NW, Suite 300
Boca Raton, FL 33487-2742

First issued in paperback 2020

© 2017 by Taylor & Francis Group, LLC
CRC Press is an imprint of Taylor & Francis Group, an Informa business

No claim to original U.S. Government works

ISBN-13: 978-1-4987-8038-4 (hbk)
ISBN-13: 978-0-367-59590-6 (pbk)

Library of Congress Cataloging-in-Publication Data

Names: Gius, Mark, author.
Title: Guns and crime : the data don't lie / Mark Gius.
Description: Boca Raton, FL : CRC Press, [2017] | Includes bibliographical references.
Identifiers: LCCN 2016019709| ISBN 9781498780384 (hardback) | ISBN 1498780385 (hardback) | ISBN 9781315450889 (web pdf) | ISBN 1315450879 (web pdf)
Subjects: LCSH: Firearms and crime--United States. | Firearms ownership--United States. | Gun control--United States. | Violent crimes--United States.
Classification: LCC HV7436 .G58 2017 | DDC 364.2--dc23
LC record available at https://lccn.loc.gov/2016019709

Visit the Taylor & Francis Web site at
http://www.taylorandfrancis.com

and the CRC Press Web site at
http://www.crcpress.com

Dedicated to my wife and my sons.
Their support and love have made this possible.

Contents

List of tables

About the author

Mark Gius, PhD, is a professor of economics at Quinnipiac University in Hamden, Connecticut. He earned his PhD in economics from the Pennsylvania State University. His teaching interests are labor economics, law and economics, and industrial organization. His main area of research interest is applied microeconomics with an emphasis on public policy research. His research has appeared in *Applied Economics*, *Applied Economic Letters*, and the *Social Science Journal*.

Introduction

My personal experience with guns

I grew up around guns. It was very common in rural Pennsylvania in the 1970s to own a gun. The attitudes toward guns were very different back then. When I was growing up, I hardly ever heard anyone speak of a constitutional right to own guns. I never heard anyone say that they needed a gun to protect their families (even though most crime rates in the 1970s were much higher than they are today). I definitely did not hear anyone say that we needed guns in order to fight a potentially tyrannical federal government. Instead, most people who owned guns used them to hunt. My dad loved to hunt, and so did I. Most of the hunting that we did was small game. We hunted rabbits, squirrels, ruffed grouse, and woodcock. We sometimes went goose hunting, and my uncle took me deer hunting a few times. My dad thought that the only proper way to hunt small game was with a dog, so, over the years, we owned a few beagles, Brittany spaniels, English pointers, and English setters. Some of my fondest memories as a teenager were hunting with my dad on beautiful fall weekends.

My dad bought a few guns for me to use when I was a teenager. My dad bought almost all of his guns at a small hardware store. One of the first guns that my dad bought me was a Marlin 39A lever-action .22-caliber rifle. It was great. Very accurate. I then decided to save up some money to buy a shotgun for bird hunting. After a whole summer of cutting lawns, I saved up $200, enough for my dad to buy me a Savage Fox 20-gauge double-barreled shotgun. It was very light and fit me great. When my dad bought the gun, there was no background check or waiting period or anything. We just walked out of the store, gun in hand. During my teenage years, my dad bought a few more guns. He bought a Marlin .30-30 rifle, a Marlin .35 Remington rifle, a double-barreled 12-gauge shotgun, and a ponderous bolt-action 12-gauge shotgun with a very long barrel that we used for goose hunting. My dad preferred to hunt with a .410 double-barreled shotgun. I still have no idea how he hit anything with that small gun, but he bagged his fair share of rabbits and birds. When I was 16 years old, my dad bought a Ruger Single-Six .22-caliber single-action revolver. It was beautiful, with a rich walnut handle and a stainless-steel finish. He even got a custom-fitted holster for the pistol.

I also took up trap shooting at the time. We used a portable trap that you would bolt to the spare tire of your car. (This is back when cars had full-size spares.) My friends and I would go through boxes of shells and cases of clay pigeons on warm Sunday afternoons. It was just great.

Then, I went away to college. Over the years, I kind of drifted away from hunting and shooting. I moved around too much, and, after I got married, my wife did not like having guns in the house, so that is when I stopped shooting and hunting. After we had kids, things changed. It had nothing to do with personal safety or a belief in the inalienability of the Second Amendment. Rather, it had mostly to do with trying to give my kids a little bit of the enjoyment that I had when I was young. So, starting a couple of years ago, whenever we went back to Pennsylvania to visit my parents, my sons and I went shooting. Most of the guns that I had used when I was a teenager were sold years ago, but my dad had kept three of them (the .22 Ruger pistol, the 20-gauge shotgun, and the .22 Marlin rifle). My sister still lives in Pennsylvania and is an active hunter, so she took us to outdoor ranges to practice shooting. I was a little nervous when my sons first started shooting, but my sister and I lectured them extensively on gun safety, and, we only put in one round at a time, so as to minimize the possibility of an accident.

After a year or so of shooting in Pennsylvania, my older son asked me if we could bring the guns that I had used as a teenager back to Connecticut. That's when I got a lesson in the new world of gun laws. I thought that it would probably be difficult to bring up my dad's guns from Pennsylvania, so I thought that the best and easiest course would be to use the range's guns. That way, I would not have to worry about permits, and my wife and I would not get into an argument about having guns in the house. Well, the shooting range I contacted squashed all of those dreams.

First, their staff told me that if I just wanted to shoot at the range, then I could take a class that is offered at their range and rent one of their pistols to use. The person from the range emphasized that I would not be able to transport a pistol of any kind or even buy ammunition. I then explained that I would like to bring my 13-year-old son to the range as well. That changed everything, I was told. In order to bring my son, I would have to obtain a Connecticut State Pistol Permit. I asked him how long it would take to obtain the permit. He said anywhere from three months to two years. I thanked him and started to do some research.

I found out that there are three different types of firearm permits in the state of Connecticut. The easiest to obtain is an ammunition certificate.

With this type of permit, you can only buy ammunition. You do not have to take any gun safety course for this type of permit. All you have to do is fill out a simple form and pay a $35 fee. The certificate is valid for five years. The state conducts an in-state criminal background check. The application and payment must be handed in at the Department of Emergency Services and Public Protection (DESPP).

The second type of permit is the certificate to purchase long guns. With this certificate, you can buy a rifle or a shotgun. There is no permit that is needed to transport a long gun in the state of Connecticut. In addition, with this certificate, you can buy ammunition. Applying for this type of permit, however, is a bit more involved than applying for an ammunition certificate. First, you have to take a firearm safety course. Most applicants take the National Rifle Association (NRA) Basic Pistol Shooting Course, although other types of NRA courses would suffice. The course lasts eight hours and costs about $100. After obtaining all of the necessary paperwork, you then have to show up at the local police department to get fingerprinted, pay the fees ($99.75), and hand in the application. If you pass the background check, then you must go to DESPP, get photographed, and obtain your permit. It is valid for five years.

Finally, there is the pistol permit. Since this permit would allow me to transport a pistol, I decided to obtain this one. I was also told at the shooting range that I needed a pistol permit if I wanted to bring my son to the range. The process of applying for a pistol permit is very similar to that of applying for a certificate to purchase a long gun. I first signed up both myself and my son for a class (NRA Basic Pistol Shooting). I emailed the instructor about a month before the course. He said that they filled up quickly, and, as soon as he had available dates, he would email me. The course cost $110. We took the course on a cold Saturday in January. The course mostly dealt with gun safety and guns in general. I wish that the instructor would not have talked about the politics of gun control (he was against it) or about how dangerous the world was, but he was very thorough and covered all of the basics of gun safety. At the end of the day, we took a 50-question test (which we graded ourselves), fired 20 rounds from a .22-caliber pistol, and obtained our certificates.

I then printed off the pistol permit application from my local police department website and began obtaining the necessary materials. One thing I noticed is that my local police department required three letters of recommendation in order to obtain a pistol permit, something that is not required by the state. I called my local police department and asked them if the letters were optional. The officer I talked to made it clear that they were required. I was not exactly sure why the letters were needed, but I got a few friends to write me letters, and I thought that the hard part was over. I then read the instructions further and found out that the police department only accepted pistol permit applications and fingerprints applicants on Sunday mornings from 9 to 11. I thought that was rather restrictive, but I showed up at the police station the following Sunday with all of the necessary paperwork. When I got there at 9 am, there were already about 10 people in line. I handed in my paperwork at the desk. After a few minutes, a police officer came out to address the small crowd waiting in the lobby. He said that the fingerprinting would take about 15–20 minutes per person and that they had only one fingerprint scanner. He did say, however, that they would stay as long as necessary in order to process all applications. I settled in for a long wait. While we were waiting, several others showed up to hand in their applications. One unfortunate individual forgot his letters of recommendation. The police did not accept his application. Finally, I was fingerprinted. They asked me a few questions in order to verify my identity. And that was it. I am now waiting for their decision regarding the pistol permit application, which may take days, weeks, or months. If approved, the police will issue me a temporary state permit to carry pistols and revolvers. I will then have 60 days to go a local DESPP office in order to obtain the actual state pistol permit. That will cost me another $70. And I had to go through all this just because I wanted to take my son to an indoor shooting range.

The following are a few observations regarding the application process:

1. *It is time consuming.* The class took eight hours, assembling the materials (birth certificate, letters of recommendation) took a few hours, and the wait in line at police headquarters took another two hours. I thought that it was a lot, especially given my prior experience with firearms.
2. *Is the training sufficient for a novice?* For somebody who has no experience with guns, eight hours of training may or may not be enough. Remember, we only shot 20 rounds of ammunition in the training. For somebody who has never handled a firearm before, that is not much practice. It is important to note that a pistol permit holder can carry a handgun both concealed and in the open (concealed carry and open carry). Do we really want somebody who only ever shot 20 rounds of ammunition from a .22 caliber pistol to be carrying a loaded firearm in public?
3. *It is expensive.* The total cost to obtain a pistol permit in Connecticut is $314.75. That includes the class fee but not the cost of other incidentals, such as the cost to obtain a certified copy of a birth certificate. And that is before you buy a gun or ammunition or any time on a range. This is an expensive hobby. It also raises the possibility that the reason some individuals may not obtain the necessary permits

is not that they have criminal or mental health histories but rather because they cannot afford the permit fees.

4. *State gun control measures are much more restrictive than federal gun control laws.* In most states, if I had wanted to take my son to a shooting range, I would not have had to go through the laborious process that I did here in Connecticut. In most states, I probably could have just showed up at the range and went shooting with my son. Granted, the range imposed its own rules, but I believe that those rules were in response to the Connecticut gun control laws. If I wanted to buy a gun in most other states, I would not have had to obtain a permit. According to federal law, if I want to buy a gun from a federally licensed firearms dealer, all I would have to do is go through a background check to see if I am legally able to purchase a firearm. The background check must be completed within three days. Most background checks are performed rather quickly, usually while the customer is waiting. Very few are denied. In fact, fewer than 2% of firearm transfers have been denied since background checks started in 1994. In most states, if I want to buy a gun from a private party, no background check is required. Obviously, it is much more difficult to buy a gun in Connecticut than it is in most other states.

5. *It is interesting to note, however, that the restrictions imposed by the local police department are somewhat more onerous than state restrictions.* For example, according to state statute, all that is required in order to obtain a pistol permit in Connecticut is a firearms safety course certificate and proof that you are legally residing in the United States (copy of passport, birth certificate, etc.). Then, you are supposed to get fingerprinted at your local police department and submit all of the necessary materials. The local police department in my town, however, added a few more restrictions. First, they wanted a copy of my birth certificate, even though the state says that, in lieu of a birth certificate, I could submit a copy of my passport. Second, the applicant must submit three letters of recommendation. This is definitely not in the state laws regarding pistol permits. In fact, on January 14, 2010, the Connecticut Board of Firearms Permit Examiners, the state appellate board for disputes regarding the issuance of firearm permits, issued a declaratory ruling that "nothing in the statute authorizes an issuing authority (local police department) to add to the requirements of the statute or to the form prescribed by the Commissioner of Public Safety at the time a person submits an application for a permit to carry pistols and revolvers." Hence, six years ago, the state appellate board for firearm permits declared that local issuing authorities cannot require additional documentation, and yet my local police department continued to do so. Finally, imposing

the restriction that pistol permit applicants can only get finger-printed and submit their applications on Sunday mornings from 9 to 11 seems rather restrictive. It appears as if the local police want to reduce the number of pistol permits that are issued in their town. If the local authorities would just follow the state statute, the process would not have been that daunting. But, by adding to the number of documents required and by having a very small time window for fingerprints and submission of applications, the local police depart-ment probably has done more to reduce the likelihood that a person would obtain a pistol permit than any federal regulation ever would.

6. *Another interesting side note concerns the rules of the shooting range.* The NRA pistol class I took was held at the shooting range that I ini-tially contacted. After my son and I finished the class, we went to the front desk and inquired about their hours of operation. We were then informed that even after I get my pistol permit, I would have to wait at least one year before I would be allowed to bring my son to the range. I found this peculiar, especially given that I have a lot of experience with firearms. He said that did not matter. I then told him that my son took the NRA class with me. He said that it still did not matter. My son and I then left, both somewhat dejected. After we got in the car, the person from the range came running up to the car, tapping on the window. I thought that I had forgotten something at the range. He told me that given my son took the course, he would be able to come to the range once I obtained my permit. I thanked him for clarifying their policy and then drove off. I still wonder what will happen the first time we show up at the range to shoot.

The reason I presented in great detail this personal narrative regard-ing my experience with firearms is that I want to address in a personal manner many of the issues and controversies surrounding guns and gun control in the United States. Although much is made about federal gun control measures, in reality, they are not very onerous. The one policy that has the most effect on the average gun owner is the background check requirement for firearm purchases. As noted earlier, most of these back-ground checks are completed while the customer is waiting, and, after three days, the sale can proceed if the background check is not completed. In addition, private sales do not require background checks. Hence, in my opinion, these requirements are rather minimal.

Connecticut gun control laws impose numerous additional restric-tions on top of the federal gun control laws. As noted above, these restric-tions are substantial. However, once a permit is obtained, there is no limit to the number of firearms or the amount of ammunition that an individ-ual can purchase. In addition, a person who has a pistol permit can carry any firearm open or concealed. And this is after only taking an eight-hour class and shooting 20 rounds from a .22-caliber handgun.

Local restrictions are sometimes more onerous than either state or federal regulations. By requiring additional documentation and having very narrow time windows for the submission of applications, local police have essentially created significant barriers to entry for potential gun owners. In addition, one aspect of gun control that has never been examined but is rather restrictive, in my opinion, is the cost of obtaining a state permit. As noted earlier, the cost to obtain a pistol permit in Connecticut is over $300. For a lower-income person, that is a rather substantial fee.

The purpose of this book is to examine prior research and statistics regarding guns, crime, and gun control. Interestingly, there are not much data on the supply of guns. Although researchers have attempted to estimate gun supplies at regional or state levels, there are no authoritative data on gun supply in the United States. This issue will be discussed in Chapter 1.

Next, this book will examine the reliability of crime data. Crime data, especially at the state and county level, are not as reliable as some would think. In addition, data on gun-related crime are especially lacking. For state-level data, only three crimes are disaggregated by the type of weapon used: (1) murder, (2) robbery, and (3) aggravated assault. Hence, we do not know what percentages of rapes are committed using a firearm at the state level. This issue will be discussed in Chapter 2.

Another area where crime data are lacking is in the area of self-protective behaviors. Self-protective behaviors are defined as victims defending themselves against criminals. We have no authoritative data on the actual number of self-protective behaviors in a given year. The only data that are available are survey data. Although this lack of data may seem trivial, it is rather important because one of the main arguments of gun control opponents is that guns must be readily available so that individuals are able to defend themselves against criminal attacks. If, however, there are little data on self-protective behaviors, then how would one examine the validity of their argument? This issue will be discussed in Chapter 3.

Gun control cannot directly affect criminal behavior. Rather, gun control studies assume that gun control laws affect the supply of guns and that the gun supply affects the level of criminal behavior that is observed. These are rather significant assumptions that are untested for the most part. Most research in this area examines state-level gun control measures. Few studies have examined local restrictions on gun control, or the effects of the costs of obtaining permits on gun ownership. A review of research in this area will be discussed in Chapter 6.

Finally, several proposals are presented in Chapter 8. These proposals address not only relevant and effective gun control measures, but also issues regarding data on gun supply, crime, and self-protective behaviors. In developing these proposals, it is important to balance an individual's Second Amendment rights against society's interest in reducing firearm violence. Too often, only extreme policies that cater to a like-minded base of support are considered acceptable, thus resulting in an unwillingness to compromise and a disinclination to consider evidence-based policies that may reduce crime while at the same time securing freedoms and liberties that are guaranteed by the Constitution.

chapter one

Guns in America

As noted in the introduction, my dad has three guns in his house. I have none. Unfortunately, that is the extent of information that I possess on the supply of guns in America. Authorities probably even know less than I do about the supply of guns in Pennsylvania. The reasons are varied. First, since there is no national registry of firearms, except for certain very dangerous weapons, there is no information on who owns what firearms in the United States. Second, although federally licensed firearms dealers are required to maintain records on every firearm transfer, they do not have to notify authorities regarding the transfers. In fact, federal law prohibits the creation of a central repository of firearm sales records (Firearm Owner's Protection Act, 1986). Second, approximately 40% of all firearm transfers are between private parties (Cook and Ludwig 1997). It is important to note that the 40% value is a rough estimate based on survey data. Given that no background checks are required for private transfers, there is no way to verify this estimate. Third, in private firearm transfers, neither the seller nor the buyer of the firearm is obligated to report the sale to the authorities. In only 11 states and the District of Columbia are sellers required to report transfers of firearms to the authorities. In five of those states, all firearm transfers must be reported. In the remainder of the states, only handgun transfers need to be reported. Fourth, although federal law requires dealers to maintain the records of firearm transfers indefinitely, background check records are destroyed quickly. All information on approved transfers must be destroyed within 24 hours upon the notification of the background check approval. Information on denials is retained by the Federal Bureau of Investigation (FBI) indefinitely.

Fifth, very few states require all firearms to be registered. Only Hawaii and the District of Columbia require that all firearms be registered. New York requires that handguns and assault weapons have to be registered, and, in California, Connecticut, Maryland, and New Jersey, only assault weapons have to be registered. Given all of the above, it is very difficult for law enforcement or any state or federal authority to determine the supply of firearms in the United States.

The only firearms in the United States that have to be registered with federal authorities are those that are covered by the National Firearms

Act (NFA) of 1934. The NFA was enacted in response to killings that were perpetrated by organized crime syndicates and other criminals, such as Al Capone. Although the intent of the law was to reduce the supply of weapons such as machine guns, shortened long guns, and silencers, the act was presented to the public and Congress as a tax bill. A $200 tax was imposed on the sale and transfer of most NFA firearms. This tax is still in existence, and it is still $200 per transfer. Given that the dollar value of the tax has not changed, the negative effect of the tax on the demand for NFA weapons has diminished somewhat.

In addition to the tax, owners of NFA firearms and weapons have to register their weapons with the Bureau of Alcohol, Tobacco, Firearms, and Explosives (BATF). In 1986, the Firearm Owners' Protection Act was passed, which amended the definition of a silencer and prohibited the transfer and possession of machine guns, except for government agencies and those machine guns that were lawfully possessed before May 19, 1986.

Given the required registration of NFA weapons, the federal government knows with a great deal of precision how many NFA weapons are currently in existence in the United States. According to the BATF, in February of 2015, there were 543,073 machine guns; 2,446,984 destructive devices, which include bombs, grenades, and mines; 792,282 silencers; 181,314 short-barreled rifles; and 138,393 short-barreled shotguns. The states with the largest number of NFA weapons are, in descending order, Texas, California, Virginia, Florida, and Pennsylvania. The states with the fewest number of NFA weapons are Rhode Island, Delaware, Vermont, Hawaii, and North Dakota.

Unfortunately, for non-NFA firearms, we do not know how many exist in the United States, let alone how many exist in each individual state or county. Most studies on gun ownership use proxy variables for gun supply. Some studies use subscription rates for gun magazines or NRA memberships (Kleck and Patterson 1993). Others use survey data (Kleck and Hogan 1999; Miller et al. 2002, 2006; Moody and Marvell 2005; Gius 2009, 2011). One study uses background checks as a proxy for gun prevalence (Lang 2013). Finally, some studies use the ratio of firearm suicides to total suicides.

It is important to note that none of these proxy variables include information on how many guns are in a given state or region. In the case of survey data, most only ask if there is a firearm in the respondent's residence. There are no survey questions regarding how many firearms a respondent owns. The other proxy measures (magazine subscriptions, NRA memberships, background checks, and firearm suicide ratios) are measures of firearm prevalence and contain no information on the number of firearms in circulation. Given that survey data provide the best information on actual gun ownership, several of the more commonly used surveys will be examined.

One of the more frequently used surveys in the gun prevalence literature is the General Social Surveys (GSS). The GSS is a survey on the demographic characteristics and social attitudes of U.S. residents and is administered by the National Opinion Research Center (NORC) located at the University of Chicago. It has been conducted annually from 1972 to 1994, except for the years 1979, 1981, and 1992, and biennially beginning in 1994. As of 2014, data on over 59,000 respondents and almost 6000 variables have been collected. The survey questions encompass a wide variety of subject matter, including the respondents' demographic information and their opinions on matters ranging from government spending to the state of race relations. The GSS uses primarily in-person interviews. With regards to firearms, several questions are asked on the GSS. The two most relevant questions are as follows:

1. "Do you happen to have in your home any guns or revolvers?"
2. "Do any of these guns personally belong to you?"

Unfortunately, there are no questions on how many firearms a respondent owns. In addition, one problem with the GSS data is the relatively small number of responses to these questions. In the 2014 survey, only 1657 individuals answered the question "Do you happen to have in your home any guns or revolvers?" Although potentially large enough for an analysis of national data, there are not enough responses to infer gun ownership at the state or regional level. The GSS is only suitable for a national or regional analysis of gun ownership. No state-level analyses should be attempted with these data.

Another commonly used survey in the gun prevalence literature is the Behavioral Risk Factor Surveillance System (BRFSS). The BRFSS is a data collection program that is administered by the Centers for Disease Control and Prevention and the U.S. states and territories. This program, which began in 1984, measures and collects data on the behavioral risk factors of adults. No question is asked regarding the number of guns in a given household. The firearm questions, which are similar to those asked in the GSS, only deal with whether or not a household has guns. The most relevant question in the BRFSS is as follows:

"Are any firearms now kept in or around your home?"

Unfortunately, the questions on firearms were only asked in seven years of the survey, the latest being 2004. Hence, the data regarding gun ownership are somewhat dated.

A seldom-used survey in the gun prevalence literature is the National Longitudinal Survey of Youth (NLSY). The NLSY was constructed to be a nationally representative sample of the civilian noninstitutionalized population at the time of the initial survey in 1979. A second survey with a different cohort was started in 1997. The 1979 NLSY consisted of 12,686 men and women between the ages of 14 and 22 when the survey was started in 1979. The 1997 NLSY consisted of 8984 men and women between the ages of 12 and 16 when the survey was started in 1997. The NLSY employs extensive household interviews in the selected sampling areas in order to obtain as random and as representative a sample as possible.

Unfortunately, there are several drawbacks regarding the use of the NLSY in gun supply research. First, not all ages are represented in the sample. In the 1997 NLSY, there is only a very narrow age range of five years. Hence, the results obtained from such a data set may not be applicable to the population in general. Second, there are no questions on gun ownership. All of the questions deal with whether the respondent carried a gun since the last interview or in the past 30 days. It is unknown if the gun was owned by the respondent, nor is it known how many guns the respondent owns. Finally, the gun questions in the NLSY elicited very few responses, thus resulting in such a small data set that most statistical analyses would be impractical.

In order to develop a more accurate measure of gun ownership, Lang (2013) used background check data as a measure of the change in the stock of firearms for a given state. This unique proxy variable for gun prevalence has its roots in the Brady Handgun Violence Prevention Act (Brady Act) of 1993. Starting in February of 1994, the federal government required all buyers of handguns to undergo a background check in order to determine if the potential buyer is legally allowed to possess a gun. The reasons why a person may fail a background check include felony convictions, felony indictments, domestic violence misdemeanors, restraining orders, fugitive status, illegal alien status, mental illness or disability, drug addiction, and local or state prohibition. From February of 1994 to November of 1998, the act only applied to handgun sales. In November of 1998, the permanent provisions of the Brady Act took effect. These permanent provisions established the National Instant Criminal Background Check System (NICS) and extended the act's provisions to purchasers of long guns and to persons who redeem pawned firearms. States have the option of conducting their own background checks, or they may have the checks performed by the FBI. From 1994 to 2009, only 1.8% of firearm sales were denied. Finally, the Brady Act does not require background checks for firearm purchases that are conducted through unlicensed firearm dealers (private sales), although several states require background checks for private sales.

In his analysis of the relationship between background checks and suicide rates, Lang (2013) used state-level data on background checks as a proxy for gun availability. The author compared this proxy variable to several more commonly used proxies and found a strong positive correlation between background checks and these more established gun supply proxies. There are, however, several issues with using this variable as a proxy: Many states do not require the registration or licensing of firearms, private gun purchases are exempt from background checks, firearm dealers may not comply with the law, and, finally, there may be private transfers of guns across state lines. Nonetheless, Lang notes that background checks measure the intent to purchase a gun and hence serve as a proxy for the change in gun availability over time.

Although it is a unique approach to estimating firearm prevalence, the primary problem with this estimating methodology is that it only provides an estimate of the change in the stock of firearms, but provides no indication about how many firearms are owned in total. Given that firearms are durable goods, guns that were sold decades ago could still be in use. Hence, looking at annual sales (background checks) only captures a very small part of the supply of firearms in the United States.

One final approach that is used to estimate the supply of firearms in the United States is the use of production and trade data on firearms. Brauer (2013), in his working paper "The U.S. Firearms Industry," examines the economic characteristics of the U.S. firearms industry. Utilizing data from the BATF, the FBI, the U.S. Customs and Border Protection, and the U.S. Census Bureau, Brauer attempts to estimate the number of firearm producers, the number of firearms produced, industry consolidation, foreign competition, international trade, and the overall market structure of the U.S. firearm industry. Using data from 1986 to 2010, the author finds that there were more than 2200 firearm producers, a net domestic production of more than 98 million (net of exports), and imports of at least 48 million. His analysis shows that for every year, during the period in question, the supply of firearms in the United States increased by 6 million units. In addition, more than 1.5 million used firearms changed hands in 2010.

It is important to note, however, that Brauer was unable to determine the actual number of firearms in the United States. The reasons for this are many but primarily are due to the lack of reliable firearm supply data. As noted earlier, there is no national registry of firearms and, given that guns are durable goods, looking at background checks or production data only provides information on the change in the supply of firearms and not on the actual number of firearms.

The one piece of information that the survey data (GSS and BRFSS) can provide us is an estimate of the percentage of persons who own a gun in the United States. For the GSS data, the relevant question is as follows:

> "Do you happen to have any guns or revolvers in your home?"

Data are presented in Figure 1.1.

According to these data, the percentage of Americans having a gun in their home was approximately 50% in the early 1970s but then dropped at a fairly steady rate until, in 2014, only 31% of Americans claimed to have a gun in their house.

In looking at the BRFSS data, the relevant question is as follows:

> "Are any firearms kept in or around your home?"

Unfortunately, the only years in which this question was asked were 1995, 1996, 1997, 1998, 2001, 2002, and 2004. The available data are presented in Figure 1.2.

The BRFSS survey findings are similar to those of the GSS data and suggest that approximately 30%–35% of Americans have a gun in their home. Unfortunately, for neither survey do we have any information on how many guns are in the respondents' homes.

In conclusion, although some prior studies have attempted to develop proxy measures of gun ownership (Kleck and Patterson 1993; Duggan 2001; Miller et al. 2002; Bugg and Yang 2004; Moody and Marvell 2005; Gius 2008), no researcher has yet been able to obtain data on actual gun ownership levels in the United States. Proxy measures used in prior research include the subscription rates of gun and hunting magazines, the number of National Rifle Association (NRA) members per 100,000 persons, firearm-related suicide rates, and national survey data (GSS

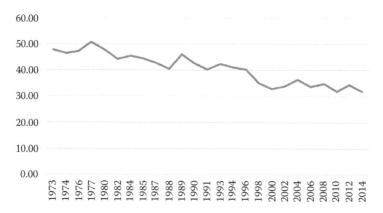

Figure 1.1 Percentage of Americans that have a gun in their home. Source: GSS.

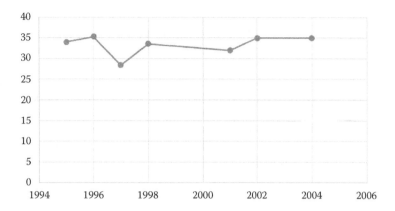

Figure 1.2 Percentage of Americans that have a gun in their home. Source: BRFSS.

and the BRFSS). Unfortunately, none of these proxies provide an adequate estimate of the number of guns in a particular state or county. Without such data, it is difficult to determine a variety of statistical relationships, including the relationship between gun ownership and gun-related crime.

Another interesting question regarding gun ownership is the issue of why some persons feel compelled to own guns and others do not. There have been several studies that have examined the determinants of gun ownership. Kalesan et al. (2016) use survey data from 2013 in order to determine if there is a relationship between social gun culture and gun ownership. The authors defined *gun culture exposure* by using responses from four survey questions. Their results suggest that there is a strong association between social gun culture and gun ownership. In other words, individuals who have family or friends who use guns are more likely to own guns themselves.

Bugg and Yang (2004) looked at trends in the gun ownership of women. Using data from the GSSs for the period 1973–2002, the authors found that gun ownership by women, has declined during the period in question. In examining the determinants of gun ownership, the authors found that older white women who are Republican and who live in rural areas are more likely to own guns than other women. In addition, better educated women are less likely to own guns, but higher-income women are more likely to own guns.

Ross (2001) looked at the effects of environmental factors on the probability that a person would own a gun. Using survey data on 2482 Illinois adults, the author found that the only neighborhood characteristic that was significantly related to individual gun ownership was the percentage of the neighborhood population that was college educated. The greater this percentage, the lower the probability of gun ownership. In addition, married whites and African-Americans living in rural areas are more likely to own guns than others.

Finally, Cao et al. (1997), using survey data from Cincinnati, Ohio, found that men who were exposed to a social gun culture as children are more likely to own guns. Individuals who own guns for protection did so because of neighborhood safety issues and a conservative crime ideology.

Even though this research on the determinants of gun ownership is important, it is still no substitute for actual data on gun prevalence in the United States. The lack of data on gun supply hinders the analysis of the impact of gun control laws on crime. Because of this lack of data on gun supply, we cannot ascertain with any precision the impact of guns on crime, nor can we determine the effects of gun control measures on the supply of firearms. Granted, the analyses of many public policies involve sample, rather than population, data. For example, sampling is used to determine the unemployment rate in a given state or city. However, an important distinction between the collection of unemployment data and the collection of data on gun supply is that employment data are collected on a regular basis by a government agency, and most researchers are in agreement regarding their accuracy and validity. Sample data on gun supply are collected on an irregular basis, and no attempt is made to ascertain the average number of firearms that are owned by Americans. Hence, this lack of reliable data on gun supply greatly hinders research on gun control, especially with regards to the role of guns in crime.

chapter two

Crime in America

Crime rates are at their lowest levels in decades. The odds of getting shot and killed in most major cities are much lower now than they were in the 1980s. Unfortunately, data on crime are not as definitive nor as accurate as one would think. Although crime data are much more exhaustive and comprehensive than firearm supply data, there are still discrepancies and inaccuracies. The primary source of crime data in the United States is the Federal Bureau of Investigation's (FBI's) Uniform Crime Report (UCR). For homicide, there are two sources of data: (1) the FBI's Supplementary Homicide Report (SHR) and (2) the Centers for Disease Control and Prevention's (CDC's) Fatal Injury Reports.

It is important to note a few things about the UCR. First, the data are collected by the FBI from state and local law enforcement agencies. These agencies voluntarily report arrest data to the FBI, which then compiles the data into various reports and data sets. Although there is no federal legal requirement to submit data to the UCR, many states require local law enforcement agencies to report crime data to the FBI. Second, the data represent arrests and crime reports by police, not convictions or guilty pleas.

Offenses are categorized in the UCR as Part I offenses and Part II offenses. Part I offenses include murder, non-negligent homicide, forcible rape, robbery, aggravated assault, burglary, larceny, motor vehicle theft, and arson. Part II offenses include lesser offenses such as embezzlement, vandalism, and prostitution. Traffic violations are not included in either Part I or Part II. For Part I offenses, the UCR collects data on the number of offenses that become known to law enforcement; the number of arrests; and the age, race, and sex of persons arrested. For Part II offenses, only arrest data are collected. The UCR does not include federal law enforcement agencies.

There are two agencies that collect data on murder and homicide: (1) the FBI and (2) the CDC. The FBI collects data through the SHR of the UCR. The SHR provides detailed information about each homicide incident, including the jurisdiction where the homicide occurred, the weapon used, the victim and offender demographic characteristics, the date of the incident, the circumstances of the incident, and the relationship between the offender and the victim. The SHR also reports homicide data by state, county, and city.

The SHR has several limitations, however. First, as noted above, federal crimes are not reported in the UCR. Thus, the SHR does not include murders on military bases, in federal prisons, and on Indian reservations. Second, homicides reported through the SHR may have missing information about the incident because the data were not available at the time of the reporting. Third, given that SHR reports are voluntary, some states provide little or no information regarding murders, and there are substantial errors in the reporting of homicides. For example, Alabama reported 341 murders in 1998, 15 in 1999, and 233 in 2000. Clearly, the 1999 value is an error. In addition, Florida did not report any murder data for the years 1988–1991 and 1997–2014. There are other obvious errors and omissions in the homicide data that were reported in the SHR, thus calling into question the validity and veracity of the data. Finally, although the FBI attempts to correct for missing observations by imputing data, they only use these imputed values to aggregate the data to the state, regional, and national level (Maltz and Targonski 2002). The FBI does not publish imputed county-level data. Hence, due to the inconsistency of these data, the use of UCR's county-level crime data for any type of analysis should be viewed with suspicion.

The other agency that reports homicide data is the CDC. The CDC reports homicide data in their Fatal Injury Reports, using data from death certificates that are reported to the National Vital Statistics System (NVSS). Death certificate data include the age at death, race, ethnicity, marital status, resident status, educational attainment, residence, the cause of death, and the nature of injuries sustained. No information is available on the offender. Over 99% of deaths are reported to the NVSS.

The CDC data also have their limitations. First, the CDC is totally dependent upon local officials (coroners and medical examiners) in correctly completing death certificates and correctly coding deaths as homicides. Second, demographic information on a death certificate is typically entered by a funeral director. Hence, there may be errors regarding certain demographic attributes, such as race and residence. Finally, although the CDC data report homicides by firearm, they do not break down firearms by type (handgun, long gun, etc.) nor do they report if the murder was connected to another crime. Unfortunately, even with all of the shortcomings of both the FBI and the CDC data, researchers and legislators must use one of these sources because there are no other murder data available.

It is now instructive to review some crime data, especially murder data, in order to dispel some myths about guns and murder and to show just how little we know about murder in the United States. This analysis will focus on those crimes that are disaggregated by the type of weapon used. Given that the FBI data are much more comprehensive in terms of the information available, only the data source in Tables 2.1 through 2.3 will be used in this analysis.

As the data on Table 2.1 illustrate, crime is at its lowest levels in decades. Murder rates are the lowest since 1963 (the earliest available data). Rape rates are the lowest since 1978. Robbery rates are the lowest since 1968. Aggravated assault rates are the lowest since 1977. Burglary rates are the lowest since 1966. Motor vehicle theft rates are the lowest since 1964. Hence, crime is rather low compared to historical standards.

As can be seen in Tables 2.2 and 2.3, the vast majority of murders were committed using firearms. In 2014, almost 68% of all murders were firearm related. Handguns were used in 46% of all murders and in 68% of firearm-related murders. Although a large minority of firearms are not identified, rifles were only used in 2% of murders, and shotguns were used in only 2.2% of murders. Unidentified firearms were used in 16.4% of murders. Hence, firearms are the most commonly used weapon in murders. State-level data on firearm usage in murders are presented on Table 2.4. In 2014, California and Texas had the most murders, although these murders were proportionally distributed throughout the states based on their populations.

Regarding the use of firearms in other crimes, it should be noted that, aside from murders, the FBI only collects data on firearm use in robberies and aggravated assaults. Data are presented on Tables 2.5 through 2.8. For aggravated assaults, firearms were used on 22.5% of incidents, and, for robberies, firearms were used in 40.3% of incidents. Firearms were used more frequently in the South and the Midwest for both aggravated assaults and robberies. No information was available on the type of firearm (handgun, shotgun, or rifle) that was used in either crime.

Regarding the racial and gender composition of murder victims (Table 2.9), 51% are African-American, and 77.3% are male. Interestingly, African-Americans only constitute 13.2% of the U.S. population. White females constitute only 13.9% of murder victims, and African-American females constitute only 7.4% of murder victims. Unfortunately, no data were collected on whether or not a firearm was involved in a victim's murder.

Regarding the circumstances surrounding murders (Table 2.10), unfortunately, many local and state agencies do not forward this information to the FBI. Hence, for 37.7% of murders in 2014, the circumstances surrounding the murders are unknown. In looking at all murders, only 15% occurred during the commission of another felony. The most commonly specified felony in which a murder occurred was robbery. In 2014, 565 murders were committed during the commission of a robbery. Only 23 victims were killed during the commission of a rape, and 371 were killed during a drug-related felony. Approximately, 46% of all murders

Table 2.1 Selected crime rates, 1960–2012: crimes per 100,000 persons

Year	Violent crime	Murder	Rape	Robbery	Aggravated assault	Property crime	Burglary	Motor vehicle theft
1960	160.9	5.1	9.6	60.1	86.1	1726.3	508.6	183
1961	158.1	4.8	9.4	58.3	85.7	1747.9	518.9	183.6
1962	162.3	4.6	9.4	59.7	88.6	1857.5	535.2	197.4
1963	168.2	4.6	9.4	61.8	92.4	2012.1	576.4	216.6
1964	190.6	4.9	11.2	68.2	106.2	2197.5	634.7	247.4
1965	200.2	5.1	12.1	71.7	111.3	2248.8	662.7	256.8
1966	220	5.6	13.2	80.8	120.3	2450.9	721	286.9
1967	253.2	6.2	14	102.8	130.2	2736.5	826.6	334.1
1968	298.4	6.9	15.9	131.8	143.8	3071.8	932.3	393
1969	328.7	7.3	18.5	148.4	154.5	3351.3	984.1	436.2
1970	363.5	7.9	18.7	172.1	164.8	3621	1084.9	456.8
1971	396	8.6	20.5	188	178.8	3768.8	1163.5	459.8
1972	401	9	22.5	180.7	188.8	3560.4	1140.8	426.1
1973	417.4	9.4	24.5	183.1	200.5	3737	1222.5	442.6
1974	461.1	9.8	26.2	209.3	215.8	4389.3	1437.7	462.2
1975	487.8	9.6	26.3	220.8	231.1	4810.7	1532.1	473.7
1976	467.8	8.7	26.6	199.3	233.2	4819.5	1448.2	450
1977	475.9	8.8	29.4	190.7	247	4601.7	1419.8	451.9

(Continued)

Table 2.1 (Continued) Selected crime rates, 1960–2012: crimes per 100,000 persons

Year	Violent crime	Murder	Rape	Robbery	Aggravated assault	Property crime	Burglary	Motor vehicle theft
1978	497.8	9	31	195.8	262.1	4642.5	1434.6	460.5
1979	548.9	9.8	34.7	218.4	286	5016.6	1511.9	505.6
1980	596.6	10.2	36.8	251.1	298.5	5353.3	1684.1	502.2
1981	593.5	9.8	36	258.4	289.3	5256.5	1647.2	474.1
1982	570.8	9.1	34	238.8	289	5029.7	1488	458.6
1983	538.1	8.3	33.8	216.7	279.4	4641.1	1338.7	431.1
1984	539.9	7.9	35.7	205.7	290.6	4498.5	1265.5	437.7
1985	558.1	8	36.8	209.3	304	4666.4	1291.7	463.5
1986	620.1	8.6	38.1	226	347.4	4881.8	1349.8	509.8
1987	612.5	8.3	37.6	213.7	352.9	4963	1335.7	531.9
1988	640.6	8.5	37.8	222.1	372.2	5054	1316.2	586.1
1989	666.9	8.7	38.3	234.3	385.6	5107.1	1283.6	634
1990	729.6	9.4	41.1	256.3	422.9	5073.1	1232.2	655.8
1991	758.2	9.8	42.3	272.7	433.4	5140.2	1252.1	659
1992	757.7	9.3	42.8	263.7	441.9	4903.7	1168.4	631.6
1993	747.1	9.5	41.1	256	440.5	4740	1099.7	606.3
1994	713.6	9	39.3	237.8	427.6	4660.2	1042.1	591.3
1995	684.5	8.2	37.1	220.9	418.3	4590.5	987	560.3

(Continued)

Table 2.1 (Continued) Selected crime rates, 1960–2012: crimes per 100,000 persons

Year	Violent crime	Murder	Rape	Robbery	Aggravated assault	Property crime	Burglary	Motor vehicle theft
1996	636.6	7.4	36.3	201.9	391	4451	945	525.7
1997	611	6.8	35.9	186.2	382.1	4316.3	918.8	505.7
1998	567.6	6.3	34.5	165.5	361.4	4052.5	863.2	459.9
1999	523	5.7	32.8	150.1	334.3	3743.6	770.4	422.5
2000	506.5	5.5	32	145	324	3618.3	728.8	412.2
2001	504.5	5.6	31.8	148.5	318.6	3658.1	741.8	430.5
2002	494.4	5.6	33.1	146.1	309.5	3630.6	747	432.9
2003	475.8	5.7	32.3	142.5	295.4	3591.2	741	433.7
2004	463.2	5.5	32.4	136.7	288.6	3514.1	730.3	421.5
2005	469	5.6	31.8	140.8	290.8	3431.5	726.9	416.8
2006	479.3	5.8	31.6	150	292	3346.6	733.1	400.2
2007	471.8	5.7	30.6	148.3	287.2	3276.4	726.1	364.9
2008	458.6	5.4	29.8	145.9	277.5	3214.6	733	315.4
2009	431.9	5	29.1	133.1	264.7	3041.3	717.7	259.2
2010	404.5	4.8	27.7	119.3	252.8	2945.9	701	239.1
2011	387.1	4.7	27	113.9	241.5	2905.4	701.3	230
2012	386.9	4.7	26.9	112.9	242.3	2859.2	670.2	229.7

Source: Uniform Crime Reports, FBI.

Table 2.2 Percentage of murders by type of weapon, 2014

	Firearms	Knives	Unknown	Hands, fists, etc.
United States	67.9%	13.1%	13.5%	5.5%
Northeast	65.3%	16.8%	13.6%	4.3%
Midwest	70.8%	9.7%	14.5%	5.0%
South	69.6%	12.0%	12.4%	6.0%
West	64.2%	15.6%	14.3%	5.9%

Source: Crime in the United States, FBI.

Table 2.3 Murders by type of weapon, 2010–2014

	2010	2011	2012	2013	2014
Total	13,164	12,795	12,888	12,253	11,961
Total firearms	8874	8653	8897	8454	8124
Handguns	6115	6251	6404	5782	5562
Rifles	367	332	298	285	248
Shotguns	366	362	310	308	262
Other guns	93	97	116	123	93
Firearms, type not stated	1933	1611	1769	1956	1959
Knives or cutting instruments	1732	1716	1604	1490	1567
Blunt objects	549	502	522	428	435
Hands, fists, feet, etc.	769	751	707	687	660
Poison	11	5	13	11	7
Explosives	4	6	8	2	6
Fire	78	76	87	94	71
Narcotics	45	33	38	53	62
Drowning	10	15	14	4	14
Strangulation	122	88	90	85	89
Asphyxiation	98	92	106	95	96
Other weapons or weapons not stated	872	858	802	850	830

Source: Crime in the United States, FBI.

were non-felony related and 24.5% occurred during an argument. Very few murders were gang related. According to the FBI data, in 2014, there were 145 gangland killings and 570 juvenile gang killings. Together, these constitute about 6% of all murders. It is important to note, however, that, for 37.7% of murders, there is no information regarding the circumstances of the killing.

Regarding the racial composition of offenders, it is important to note that the number of arrests is less than the number of incidents reported.

Table 2.4 State-level murders by type of firearm, 2014

	Total firearms	Handguns	Rifles	Shotguns	Unknown-type firearm
Alabama	1	1	0	0	0
Alaska	22	6	0	2	14
Arizona	153	116	6	6	25
Arkansas	111	55	3	10	43
California	1169	763	40	43	323
Colorado	91	60	3	2	26
Connecticut	51	19	0	3	29
Delaware	39	29	0	0	10
District of Columbia	73	30	0	1	42
Georgia	416	371	11	10	24
Hawaii	1	1	0	0	0
Idaho	15	10	0	2	3
Illinois	371	364	5	1	1
Indiana	222	166	5	3	48
Iowa	27	10	1	3	13
Kansas	56	22	4	4	26
Kentucky	112	85	1	5	21
Louisiana	319	189	9	13	108
Maine	6	2	0	4	0
Maryland	208	190	1	6	11
Massachusetts	81	33	0	0	48
Michigan	342	209	5	4	124
Minnesota	42	33	1	3	5
Mississippi	122	97	2	3	20
Missouri	314	166	24	5	119
Montana	17	12	0	2	3
Nebraska	32	24	3	4	1
Nevada	94	14	1	0	79
New Hampshire	6	3	2	0	1
New Jersey	243	200	3	5	35
New Mexico	53	21	2	2	28
New York	344	283	1	12	48
North Carolina	318	242	21	14	41
North Dakota	6	1	1	0	4

(Continued)

Table 2.4 (Continued) State-level murders by type of firearm, 2014

	Total firearms	Handguns	Rifles	Shotguns	Unknown-type firearm
Ohio	277	180	0	4	93
Oklahoma	104	88	5	5	6
Oregon	39	16	2	2	19
Pennsylvania	453	350	8	14	81
Rhode Island	12	5	0	1	6
South Carolina	219	138	8	11	62
South Dakota	6	0	0	0	6
Tennessee	246	160	7	2	77
Texas	765	483	33	28	221
Utah	36	25	4	2	5
Vermont	6	3	2	0	1
Virginia	228	119	9	10	90
Washington	94	54	6	4	30
West Virginia	16	12	1	0	3
Wisconsin	117	79	8	2	28
Wyoming	8	6	0	1	1

Source: Crime in the United States, FBI.

Table 2.5 Percentage of aggravated assaults by type of weapon, 2014

	Firearms	Knives	Blunt weapons	Hands, fists, etc.
United States	22.5%	18.8%	31.9%	26.9%
Northeast	14.6%	22.8%	30.8%	31.8%
Midwest	25.1%	16.7%	28.4%	29.8%
South	26.7%	18.8%	32.3%	22.2%
West	18.1%	17.6%	34.0%	30.3%

Source: Crime in the United States, FBI.

There are two important reasons for this. First, some crimes are never solved. Hence, no one is ever arrested for the crime, and no arrest is reported to the FBI. Second, not all crimes are solved in the year in which they were committed. Some persons who were arrested in 2014 committed their crimes years earlier.

It is also important to note that arrests are not the final disposition of the cases. In some situations, a person arrested for a particular crime is later released by the police or is found to be not guilty. Nonetheless, their arrest is still reported to the FBI as an *arrest*. Also, no data are collected on

Table 2.6 State-level aggravated assaults by type of weapon, 2014

State	Total	Firearms	Knives	Blunt weapons	Hands, fists, etc.
Alabama	11,707	2213	1640	6353	1501
Alaska	3224	599	601	895	1129
Arizona	11,240	2773	2090	2876	3501
Arkansas	9514	2822	1340	1790	3562
California	91,654	15,776	14,853	32,465	28,560
Colorado	10,112	2713	2497	2508	2394
Connecticut	4460	617	1044	1587	1212
Delaware	2865	861	605	1036	363
District of Columbia	4125	863	1246	1419	597
Florida	61,404	15,087	11,010	21,625	13,682
Georgia	19,955	6433	3234	5331	4957
Hawaii	336	1	36	137	162
Idaho	2370	376	443	743	808
Illinois	1287	552	186	248	301
Indiana	12,994	2438	1472	3503	5581
Iowa	5897	751	932	1154	3060
Kansas	6491	2073	1386	1829	1203
Kentucky	4382	1063	740	1610	969
Louisiana	13,277	3864	2206	3650	3557
Maine	887	58	143	210	476
Maryland	11,428	1715	3029	3877	2807
Massachusetts	17,282	1897	4116	7952	3317
Michigan	26,887	7435	5309	9231	4912
Minnesota	6717	1208	1227	1719	2563
Mississippi	2337	785	303	517	732
Missouri	18,377	5472	2527	5132	5246
Montana	2194	322	318	677	877
Nebraska	3105	550	515	1055	985
Nevada	10,462	1714	2006	4533	2209
New Hampshire	1366	227	348	300	491
New Jersey	11,036	2080	2354	3428	3174
New Mexico	8620	1861	1523	2591	2645
New York	45,003	5494	11,783	12,984	14,742
North Carolina	19,414	7220	3565	4644	3985

(*Continued*)

Table 2.6 (Continued) State-level aggravated assaults by type of weapon, 2014

State	Total	Firearms	Knives	Blunt weapons	Hands, fists, etc.
North Dakota	1353	46	183	276	848
Ohio	12,920	3757	2446	4077	2640
Oklahoma	10,641	2044	2008	3525	3064
Oregon	5008	574	974	1755	1705
Pennsylvania	21,744	4399	3379	4958	9008
Rhode Island	1397	290	377	455	275
South Carolina	14,401	5033	2645	3628	3095
South Dakota	1999	213	505	445	836
Tennessee	29,523	9425	5530	10,237	4331
Texas	61,945	14,890	13,125	20,693	13,237
Utah	2609	529	679	912	489
Vermont	359	46	67	50	196
Virginia	9259	2325	1801	2688	2445
Washington	11,464	1720	1953	4154	3637
West Virginia	3317	682	449	907	1279
Wisconsin	9648	2554	1182	2005	3907
Wyoming	856	91	156	242	367

Source: Crime in the United States, FBI.

Table 2.7 Percentage of robberies by type of weapon, 2014

	Firearms	Knives	Other weapons	Strong arm
Total	40.3%	7.9%	8.8%	43.0%
Northeast	31.1%	9.8%	7.8%	51.2%
Midwest	45.3%	5.8%	9.0%	39.9%
South	49.9%	6.7%	8.3%	35.0%
West	29.3%	9.5%	10.2%	51.0%

Source: Crime in the United States, FBI.

whether or not a firearm was involved in the crime for which the person was arrested.

Table 2.11 presents data on the race of arrestees. In 2014, 51.3% of those arrested for murder, 30% of those arrested for rape, and 55% of those arrested for robbery were African-American. It is important to remember that African-Americans constitute only 13.2% of the U.S. population. Hence, African-Americans are disproportionately both the offenders and the victims of crime in the United States.

Table 2.8 State-level robberies by type of weapon, 2014

State	Total	Firearm	Knives	Other weapons	Strong arm
Alabama	4004	2581	145	299	979
Alaska	627	144	54	58	371
Arizona	4428	1614	505	362	1947
Arkansas	1855	964	93	186	612
California	48,599	13,533	4548	4817	25,701
Colorado	3017	1091	254	384	1288
Connecticut	3155	1079	315	247	1514
Delaware	1267	547	105	100	515
District of Columbia	3497	1285	291	207	1714
Florida	21,576	8634	1458	1900	9584
Georgia	11,399	6761	409	1039	3190
Hawaii	80	8	7	16	49
Idaho	193	60	29	31	73
Illinois	412	209	13	24	166
Indiana	6600	3354	387	488	2371
Iowa	1031	344	112	117	458
Kansas	1254	591	108	74	481
Kentucky	3321	1596	259	327	1139
Louisiana	4964	2652	200	308	1804
Maine	304	51	43	49	161
Maryland	7570	3304	742	507	3017
Massachusetts	5933	1601	1173	664	2495
Michigan	7902	3758	446	639	3059
Minnesota	3683	1177	271	552	1683
Mississippi	1633	1044	83	145	361
Missouri	5583	2729	338	382	2134
Montana	185	52	26	30	77
Nebraska	1014	478	71	74	391
Nevada	5951	2235	461	619	2636
New Hampshire	516	128	71	56	261
New Jersey	10,330	3684	792	616	5238
New Mexico	2072	907	263	197	705
New York	23,948	5681	2274	2065	13,928
North Carolina	7585	3897	550	678	2460

(Continued)

Table 2.8 (Continued) State-level robberies by type of weapon, 2014

State	Total	Firearm	Knives	Other weapons	Strong arm
North Dakota	171	49	18	31	73
Ohio	11,779	4702	579	1106	5392
Oklahoma	3036	1437	250	227	1122
Oregon	1958	422	234	181	1121
Pennsylvania	13,436	5710	959	798	5969
Rhode Island	528	160	76	63	229
South Carolina	3362	1830	238	240	1054
South Dakota	194	61	32	36	65
Tennessee	7241	4055	414	800	1972
Texas	29,606	15,248	2219	2306	9833
Utah	1011	263	155	125	468
Vermont	60	14	16	7	23
Virginia	4273	2189	355	366	1363
Washington	5602	1258	481	666	3197
West Virginia	410	150	58	64	138
Wisconsin	4998	2753	204	447	1594
Wyoming	53	18	3	8	24

Source: Crime in the United States, FBI.

Table 2.9 Murder victims by race, ethnicity, and sex, 2014

		Sex		
	Total	Male	Female	Unknown
Total	11,961	9246	2681	34
White	5397	3733	1664	0
Black	6095	5209	881	5
Other race	309	208	100	1
Unknown race	160	96	36	28
Hispanic or Latino	1871	1510	361	0
Not Hispanic or Latino	6764	5145	1616	3
Unknown	1913	1475	420	18

Source: Crime in the United States, FBI.

Table 2.10 Murder circumstances, 2010–2014

	2010	2011	2012	2013	2014
Total	13,164	12,795	12,888	12,253	11,961
Felony type total:	1974	1842	1842	1909	1789
Rape	41	16	16	20	23
Robbery	803	750	656	686	565
Burglary	85	95	91	94	77
Larceny-theft	21	12	15	16	21
Motor vehicle theft	35	23	22	27	25
Arson	35	38	32	37	22
Prostitution and commercialized vice	5	3	6	13	19
Other sex offenses	14	10	13	9	3
Narcotic drug laws	474	397	375	386	371
Gambling	7	8	7	7	10
Other—not specified	454	490	609	614	653
Suspected felony type	68	62	137	122	83
Other than felony type total:	6485	6056	6320	5782	5583
Romantic triangle	90	88	98	69	85
Child killed by babysitter	36	38	26	30	37
Brawl due to influence of alcohol	122	113	84	93	71
Brawl due to influence of narcotics	60	121	65	59	61
Argument over money or property	187	156	152	133	144
Other arguments	3280	3163	3147	2889	2786
Gangland killings	181	149	152	138	145
Juvenile gang killings	675	526	722	584	570
Institutional killings	17	22	13	15	18
Sniper attack	3	1	1	6	3
Other—not specified	1834	1679	1860	1766	1663
Unknown	4637	4835	4589	4440	4506

Source: Crime in the United States, FBI.

In conclusion, crime data in the United States are not as precise nor as accurate as some would believe. Given that the FBI is totally dependent on state and local agencies to provide information on both incidents of crime and arrests, there are mistakes and gaps in the data, with some states not reporting crime data for years. In addition, contrary to what many believe, murders are not heavily concentrated in particular states or cities. Instead, they are proportionally distributed based on population throughout the

Table 2.11 Arrested persons by race and crime, 2014

	Total	White	African-American	American-Indian or Alaska Native	Asian	Native Hawaiian or other Pacific Islander
Total arrests	8,730,665	6,056,687	2,427,683	135,599	100,067	10,629
Murder and non-negligent manslaughter	8230	3807	4224	83	107	9
Rape	16,326	10,977	4888	212	222	27
Robbery	74,077	31,354	41,379	616	617	111
Aggravated assault	291,600	185,612	96,511	4372	4507	598
Burglary	186,794	126,242	56,504	1703	1999	346
Larceny-theft	971,199	671,260	271,788	15,869	11,355	927
Motor vehicle theft	53,456	35,551	16,391	668	677	169
Arson	7298	5338	1709	142	98	11
Violent crime	390,233	231,750	147,002	5283	5453	745
Property crime	1,218,747	838,391	346,392	18,382	14,129	1453

Source: Crime in the United States, FBI.

various states. Most murders, also, were not committed during the commission of another, crime nor were they committed during a gang-related confrontation. Instead, most murders occur during arguments. Finally, whites are very unlikely to be involved in a murder. Most murder victims and most persons arrested for murder are African-American. It is unknown if firearms are used more or less frequently in murders involving either African-American victims or African-American offenders.

Given this lack of reliable data, it is difficult to determine with any degree of accuracy the effects of gun control and other crime-reduction methods on crime rates. Given that the only alternative source of homicide data is the CDC, this is an issue of concern. More emphasis should be focused on improving the collection of data on criminal incidents, including linking incident and arrest data along with conviction data. In addition, the reporting of firearm use in crimes should be expanded to include all crimes and should also be linked to the demographic profiles of both victims and offenders. In order to determine the significance and efficacy of gun control laws, it is important to use the most reliable and complete data so as not to make important public policy decisions based on tainted evidence and flawed empirical results.

Chapter 3 will review the data, statistics, and research that are associated with justifiable homicides and self-protective behaviors (self-defense). This is an important topic for several reasons. First, justifiable homicides, both by police and by private citizens, are typically high-profile killings, and it is important to determine the frequency with which such homicides occur. Second, it is important to examine the validity and reliability of justifiable homicide data. As will be shown in Chapter 3, the data on justifiable homicides are rather incomplete and are not disaggregated by race, sex, or the disposition of the case. Hence, it is unknown, for example, if African-Americans are more likely than whites to be the victims in justifiable homicides or if private citizens are frequently arrested and/or convicted in justifiable homicide cases. Third, it is important to examine the data and research on justifiable homicides in order to determine if castle doctrine or stand-your-ground laws have contributed to an increase in justifiable homicides. Finally, data on self-protective behaviors are very important because one of the main reasons typically put forth for having the right to keep and bear arms is self-defense. Many believe that having the ability to defend one's life, family, and property is one of the benefits of having a Second Amendment. Unfortunately, there are not much reliable data on the total number of self-protective behaviors, and there is not much agreement on the validity of one of the most commonly used data sets that contain information on self-protective behaviors. All of these issues will be examined in the following chapter.

chapter three

Justifiable homicides in America

There have been numerous incidents over the past several years involving justifiable homicides. Many of these incidents involved unarmed alleged criminals being shot by armed citizens who claimed a right of self-defense due to perceived threatening behaviors on the part of the alleged criminal. Others involved police who shot and killed armed or unarmed civilians. Many of these cases involved a white shooter and an African-American victim (Jonsson 2013; Gius 2016).

Persons who are involved in justifiable homicides are typically reacting to some form of threatening behavior. Self-defensive behaviors, such as brandishing a weapon or running, are known as self-protective behaviors. Most self-protective behaviors do not result in the offender's death. According to the report "Firearm Violence, 1993–2011," for the period 2007–2011, there were over 7.7 million instances of self-protective behaviors, but, for the same period, there were only 1343 justifiable homicides by civilians (Plant and Truman 2013).

In order to understand the concept of justifiable homicide, it is first necessary to understand the different types of self-defense laws and traditions. For many years, most states and the federal government allowed a victim to defend themselves only under certain limited circumstances. Typically, the use of force was only allowed in response to an immediate threat and the prospect of immediate physical harm. Verbal abuse was not considered threatening. In addition, the force used in self-defense had to be proportionate. If a person was physically threatened with deadly force, then they may have responded with deadly force. If, however, a person was physically threatened, but the threat was not deadly, then the victim could not use deadly force to defend themselves. Also, self-defense typically required that the victim had a *duty to retreat*. This means that if a victim could have escaped the harm in some way (run away, give up their wallet, etc.), then they could not use force, and especially deadly force, to defend themselves (Gius 2016).

Some states felt that these conditions on self-defensive behaviors were too restrictive, and so many states adopted castle doctrine laws. In general, these laws removed the duty-to-retreat condition for certain situations, usually if a victim was defending their home. Hence, a victim could use deadly force, and did not have to retreat, if a criminal tried to forcibly enter the victim's house. There are other situations when a victim could use deadly force to defend their property and their life, but the legality of the use of deadly force in these situations vary from state to state. Most states have some form of castle doctrine law.

The third type of self-defense doctrine is stand-your-ground (SYG). These laws define the parameters of a justifiable homicide that is committed by a private citizen. These parameters typically include no duty to retreat and the right to use deadly force if one feels physically threatened. Although, as noted earlier, the victims of crimes, in most states, have always had the right to defend themselves in their homes, SYG laws extend this right of self-defense to outside the home. It is important to note, that SYG rights are not unlimited. The victim has to prove that a reasonable person would have felt threatened in such a situation, and, in most states, persons involved in criminal activities cannot invoke an SYG defense. A list of states that have SYG statutes is presented in Table 3.1 (Gius 2016).

SYG laws are more controversial than common self-defense or castle doctrine laws for several reasons. First, even though most SYG laws do not explicitly endorse the use of firearms as self-protective weapons, the National Rifle Association and other conservative groups were in the forefront of advocating for such laws (Fisher and Eggen 2012). These organizations saw SYG laws as a natural extension of Second Amendment rights in that individuals who use firearms to defend themselves would be protected from prosecution. Second, many people believe that SYG laws are racially biased and that whites are more successful in invoking SYG defenses than African-Americans are. Many of the SYG cases that came to national prominence involved a white shooter and an African-American victim. Evidence on the racial disparities of SYG incidents is mixed, with some analyses showing that African-Americans are more likely to be prosecuted in an SYG incident than whites, whereas other analyses show that there is no racial difference in SYG encounters (Jonsson 2013). Finally, there is disagreement about the potential impact of SYG statutes. Many believe that SYG laws may increase the number of justifiable homicides. They feel that SYG laws escalate already tense situations and turn what may have been a minor altercation into a shooting and possibly a death. Others believe, however, that due to SYG laws, criminals are less likely to threaten individuals if the criminals know that citizens can defend themselves anywhere and with any means necessary. Hence, some believe that SYG laws may serve as a deterrent to criminal activity (Gius 2016).

There is no strong consensus on the motivation for SYG laws. McClellan and Tekin (2012, p. 4) note that "…proponents of SYG laws argue that they would have a deterrent effect on crime." However, Cheng and Hoekstra (2012, p. 7) state that "…the main rationale for these laws

Table 3.1 States with SYG laws

State	Year enacted	State	Year enacted
Alabama	2006	Missouri	2007
Alaska	2006	Montana	2009
Arizona	2006	Nevada	2005
Florida	2005	New Hampshire	2011
Georgia	2006	North Carolina	2011
Illinois	2004	North Dakota	2007
Indiana	2006	Oklahoma	2006
Kansas	2006	Pennsylvania	2011
Kentucky	2006	South Carolina	2006
Louisiana	2006	Tennessee	2007
Michigan	2006	Texas	2007
Mississippi	2006	Utah	2000
		West Virginia	2008

Source: Gius, Mark. The relationship between stand-your-ground laws and crime: A state-level analysis. *Social Science Journal*, 2016; McClellan, Chandler and Erdal Tekin, Stand your ground laws, homicides, and injuries, NBER working paper 18187, 2012; and the National Rifle Association.

Note: If the above references contradicted one another, the author examined the original state law in order to determine if a state had an SYG law.

was to provide additional leeway to potential victims in self-defense situations, not to deter crime." Even though there is disagreement about the motivation behind the enactment of these laws, it is generally assumed that these laws will have some effect on crime. If citizens are utilizing their rights under these SYG laws appropriately, then there may be a drop in crime rates and a potential increase in justifiable shootings and homicides. In addition, since the alleged criminal in an SYG situation does not have to be armed, it is reasonable to assume that all crime rates, not just gun-related crime rates, may be affected by SYG laws. If, however, citizens are exercising their rights under SYG laws inappropriately, then we may observe an increase in gun-related murders (Gius 2016).

Research on SYG laws has been limited. Chamlin (2014) used monthly data for the period 2002–2011 in order to determine if Arizona's enactment of an SYG statute would significantly affect aggravated assault and robbery rates. Using an autoregressive integrated moving average (ARIMA) interrupted time series technique, the author found that Arizona's SYG law had no effect on aggravated assaults but resulted in an increase in both armed and weaponless robberies. In addition, Chamlin found that, whereas the SYG law had no effect on homicides, it did result in an increase in suicides. Hence, this study concluded that Arizona's SYG law resulted in the opposite of what was intended. Instead of reducing crime, the SYG law in Arizona resulted in an increase in all types of robberies and even an increase in suicides. Even though this law did not change any legal requirements for the ownership of firearms, Chamlin claimed that the SYG statute increased the *availability* of firearms, thus resulting in more crime and suicides. It is unclear, however, why weaponless robberies would increase if firearms became more available (Gius 2016).

Cheng and Hoekstra (2012) examined the SYG laws and their effects on homicides and violent crime. The authors attempted to determine if SYG laws deterred violent crimes, primarily because they assumed that these types of laws increase the expected cost of committing a crime to criminals. Using state-level data from the Uniform Crime Reports (UCR) and the Supplementary Homicide Reports for the period 2000–2010, the authors found that SYG laws do not deter burglary, robbery, or aggravated assault but that they did lead to an 8% increase in the number of reported murders and non-negligent homicides. Thus, SYG laws actually resulted in more homicides; the authors note that this is probably due to the fact that SYG laws reduce the expected cost of using lethal force in order to thwart a crime. Given that the cost is lower, more potential victims are using lethal force, thus resulting in an increase in homicides (Gius 2016).

Ren et al. (2012) examined the effect of a Texas SYG statute on burglaries in Dallas and Houston. Using daily data for the period January 1, 2007–August 31, 2008 and an ARIMA model, the authors found that the passage of the law in and of itself had no statistically significant effect on burglaries in either city. However, after a well-publicized incident involving an SYG-related shooting in Houston in November of 2007, the authors found that both residential and commercial burglaries fell in Houston. The incident had no significant effect on burglaries in Dallas. Ren et al. (2012) claimed that the shooting incident created such a tremendous amount of publicity for the SYG law in Houston that would-be criminals became more aware of the law and thus curtailed their activities somewhat.

McClellan and Tekin (2012) found that SYG laws resulted in an increase in homicides. Using state-level data from the U.S. Vital Statistics for the period 2000–2010, the authors found that SYG laws were associated with a significant increase in the homicide rate of white males but that these laws had no significant effects on African-American homicides. In fact, because of SYG laws, between 28 and 33 additional white males were killed each month. Hence, these results also suggest that SYG laws do not deter crime but rather result in an increase in homicides (Gius 2016).

As can be seen in Tables 3.1 through 3.4, justifiable homicides are not as common as many believe. In 2014, the police killed 444 felons in the line of duty, and private citizens killed 277 felons during the commission of a felony. In addition, the vast majority of justifiable homicides were

Table 3.2 Justifiable homicides by type of weapon, law enforcement, 2010–2014

Year	Total	Firearms	Knives	Other weapons	Hands, fists, etc.
2010	397	396	0	1	0
2011	404	401	2	0	1
2012	426	423	0	3	0
2013	471	467	0	3	1
2014	444	442	1	1	0

Source: Crime in the United States, FBI.

Table 3.3 Justifiable homicides by type of weapon, private citizen, 2010–2014

Year	Total	Firearms	Knives	Other weapons	Hands, fists, etc.
2010	285	236	33	11	5
2011	270	209	49	9	3
2012	315	263	35	6	11
2013	286	227	35	13	11
2014	277	229	36	2	10

Source: Crime in the United States, FBI.

Table 3.4 Justifiable homicides by type of firearm, private citizen, 2010–2014

Year	Firearms	Handguns	Rifles	Shotguns	Firearms, unknown type
2010	236	170	8	30	28
2011	209	156	13	11	29
2012	263	198	20	15	30
2013	227	174	6	11	36
2014	229	178	10	10	31

Source: Crime in the United States, FBI.

committed using a gun, and the most common type of gun used by private citizens was a handgun.

There is no state-by-state breakdown of these data. There are no data on criminals that were wounded but not killed, nor are there any data on self-protective behaviors that did not result in either an injury or a death. Finally, it is unknown how many private citizens (victims) were killed in their attempt to ward off a criminal.

The average number of justifiable homicides per state in any given year is less than 10. In addition, the two most commonly used sources of crime data, (1) the Centers for Disease Control and Prevention and (2) the U.S. Department of Justice, both stress that caution must be exercised when using state-level data on justifiable homicides. Given the small number of justifiable homicides in any given state, it is very difficult to conduct statistical analyses on the effects of self-defense laws, castle doctrine laws, or SYG laws on justifiable homicides. This is unfortunate because, without such research, it is nearly impossible to determine if castle doctrine laws or SYG laws may result in more justifiable homicides. The reason for this is because SYG laws, and possibly castle doctrine laws, may reduce the expected cost of using lethal force to thwart a crime. Hence, it may be that crime victims in SYG states are more likely to use lethal force, thus resulting in an increase in justifiable homicides. Unfortunately, this cannot be determined given the small number of justifiable homicides in any given state for a given year.

Another way to determine if SYG or castle doctrine laws reduce the perceived cost of using lethal force to thwart a crime is to examine the number of self-protective behaviors engaged in by potential victims. Unfortunately, there is disagreement regarding the validity of the available data on this subject. Law enforcement agencies do not collect data on the number of self-protective behaviors engaged in by victims.

The only regularly available data on self-protective behaviors are from the National Crime Victimization Survey (NCVS). This survey has been collecting data on personal and household victimizations since 1973. The sample consists of 49,000 households and over 100,000 individuals. The NCVS is conducted every six months so that individuals are better able to recall the details that are associated with any crime experiences. The survey is administered by the U.S. Census Bureau on behalf of the Bureau of Justice Statistics. The NCVS is designed to be a national study of crime victimization. In certain years, some states have no respondents participating in the NCVS. Hence, NCVS data cannot be used to examine state-level trends in criminal victimizations or self-protective behaviors.

Some researchers and commentators, however, believe that the NCVS is flawed and that the data obtained from this survey grossly underestimate the total number of self-protective behaviors that occur annually in the United States. Two such researchers published a study on self-protective behaviors in 1995. In this study, Kleck and Gertz (1995) state that the NCVS is inaccurate because its estimate for self-protective behaviors is much less than that found in other surveys. According to Kleck and Gertz (1995), the NCVS data indicate that only 0.09 of 1% of U.S. households defensively use a firearm in any one year. Other surveys suggest that the rate of defensive gun use is up to nine times greater than that estimated from NCVS data. Many of the surveys that Kleck and Gertz examined were conducted in the

1970s, 1980s, or 1990s. Most of the surveys had indefinite recall periods for the survey participants. In other words, participants were asked if they had ever used a gun in self-defense. This may limit the ability of participants to recall the details of their experiences, thus resulting in questionable responses regarding the frequency of the use of firearms in self-defense. Finally, Kleck and Gertz admit that the focus of most of these prior surveys was not defensive firearm use. In fact, most surveys asked only one or two questions on the use of firearms in a self-defense situation.

Kleck and Gertz (1995) also questioned the survey methodology that was employed by the Census Bureau. They claim that the Census Bureau methodology encourages respondents to misrepresent and underreport the number of firearm self-protective behaviors that they were involved in. Kleck and Gertz (1995) claim that by telling respondents that the survey is being conducted for the U.S. Department of Justice, and by requiring respondents to tell the Census Bureau their name, address, and other identifying information, NCVS respondents may underreport their defensive firearm use for fear that the information may be used to convict them of a crime. This is an incorrect assertion on the part of Kleck and Gertz. On the NCVS questionnaires, it clearly states that, according to federal law, the information obtained from the survey can only be used for statistical purposes and that all information is kept confidential.

Kleck and Gertz (1995) also claim that the NCVS never asks if a respondent used a gun for self-defense and that the NCVS only asks self-protection questions if the respondent has already indicated that they were a victim of a crime. Hence, the authors claim that these surveying techniques contribute to the underreporting of incidents of defensive firearm use.

Regarding these criticisms of the NCVS, it is true that a crime incident report is only completed if the respondent believes that he or she was the victim of a crime. However, self-defensive actions can only be used if the victim felt threatened and he or she believed that he or she was the victim of a crime. Hence, it is not necessary or logical to inquire about self-protective behaviors for those respondents who say that they were not the victim of a crime.

In addition, it is a quite common survey design technique to have lead-in questions regarding particular behaviors. It does not make sense to ask someone if they engaged in a self-protective behavior if they were not the victim of a criminal act. By the very definition of self-defense, a person cannot defend themselves if they were not the victim of a crime. Therefore, surveys use lead-in questions in order to avoid confusion during the survey and to keep contradictory responses to a minimum.

In the latest NCVS questionnaire, there are a series of questions that are asked about self-protective behaviors. These questions are as follows:

41a. "Did you do anything with the idea of protecting YOURSELF or your PROPERTY while the incident was going on?" If yes, go to 42. If no, go to 41b.
41b. "Was there anything you did or tried to do about the incident while it was going on?" If yes, go to 42. If no, go to 47, which is not a question on self-protective behaviors.
42a. "What did you do?"
42b. "Please specify."
42c. "Was the respondent injured in this incident?"
43a. "Did you take these actions before, after, or at the same time that you were injured?"
43b. "Did any of your actions help the situation in any way?"
44a. "How were they helpful?"
44b. "Please specify."
45a. "Did any of your actions make the situation worse?"
46a. "How did they make the situation worse?"
46b. "Please specify."

As Kleck and Gertz noted, there are no questions that specifically inquire about the self-defensive use of a firearm. Most of the self-protective questions are rather open ended. When a respondent is asked, "What did you do?" with regards to self-protective behaviors, the interviewer has a list of actions that the victim may have engaged in. The interviewer must list all behaviors that the respondent recalls. Hence, for example, if a respondent says that he or she hit the attacker and then ran away, both of those behaviors must be noted on the survey. Hence, there are many more self-protective behaviors that are reported than there are incidents.

In order to find additional evidence to dispute the results of the NCVS, Kleck and Gertz (1995) conducted a survey on criminal victimizations in the spring of 1993. Their sample consisted of 4977 individuals and was nationally representative and stratified by state. By comparison, the NCVS sample consists of about 100,000 persons who are surveyed every six months.

The most relevant question in the Kleck and Gertz survey regarding defensive firearm use was the following:

"Within the past five years, have you yourself or another member of your household used a gun, even if it was not fired, for self-protection or for the protection of property at home, work, or elsewhere?" (Kleck and Gertz 1995, p. 161).

If the respondent answered yes to this question, and if it was to protect against a person, then the following questions were asked:

"How many incidents involving defensive uses of guns against persons happened to members of your household in the past five years?"

"Did this incident happen in the past 12 months?" (Kleck and Gertz 1995, p. 161).

One glaring problem with these questions is the issue of respondent recall. Attempting to recall incidents over the past five years may be problematic and may result in significant underreporting or overreporting of defensive firearm use. That is why the NCVS is conducted every six months. In addition by not ascertaining whether or not the respondent was the victim of a crime respondents may be recalling incidents when they illegally used a firearm. Therefore, it may be that the respondents could not recall the correct number of defensive firearm incidents over the past five years or that they recalled incidents that were not actually incidents of self-defense. Both issues may result in significant overreporting of defensive firearm use.

Please see Table 3.5 for a comparison of the results regarding self-protective behaviors that were obtained from the NCVS and Kleck and Gertz survey. As one can see from this table, the percentage of individuals who engaged in defensive firearm use is very similar for the NCVS and the Kleck and Gertz survey. The primary difference is in how they are interpreted and in how these percentages are applied. The NCVS results are only for those persons who were actually involved in a criminal incident. For 1993, according to the NCVS, 19% of respondents were involved in a criminal incident, 16% of persons involved in a criminal incident attempted to defend themselves, and 10.3% of those persons who attempted to defend themselves used a gun in some fashion. Although the 10.3% value seems high, that is only 1.6% of the persons who were involved in a criminal incident. The FBI reported in 1993 that there were 1,926,017 violent crimes and 12,218,777 property crimes. Assuming that a gun is just as likely to be used in a property crime as it would be in a violent crime (even though for some of the property crimes, the victim would not even be present), and, using the estimate of 1.6% of persons involved in a criminal incident using a gun, one obtains an estimate of 226,317 defensive firearm uses in 1993.

Table 3.5 Comparison of NCVS and Kleck and Gertz surveys, 1993

	NCVS	Kleck and Gertz
Percentage of persons who were involved in a criminal incident and who threatened criminal with gun	1.2%	**
Percentage of persons who were involved in a criminal incident and who attacked criminal with gun	0.4%	**
Defensive gun use (%)	**	1.326%

Kleck and Gertz, however, arrived at the much higher value of 2.2–2.5 million incidents of defensive firearm use in 1993. The method they used to obtain this value was to multiply the estimated adult resident population of the United States in 1993, age 18 and older, by 1.326%, the percentage of persons in the sample who said that they used a firearm defensively in the past year. I believe that this is a flawed methodology for several reasons. First, not everybody in the United States owns a firearm. In fact, using General Social Survey's (GSS's) data, it is estimated that 42.4% of U.S. households in 1993 had a firearm in their home. Hence, almost 60% of the population should have been eliminated from their calculation. Second, the very definition of a self-protective behavior is that a person is defending themselves against a criminal attack. If you were not defending yourself, then it was not a self-protective behavior. The percentage of persons who are victims of criminal attacks is rather low in any given year. In 1993, it was about 5.5%. This is based on data on the UCR about reported incidents to the police. If we use the NCVS estimate of 19% of persons in the United States who were involved in a criminal incident in 1993, which is much greater than the UCR estimate, then the correct estimate of persons using guns defensively in 1993 is as follows:

190,538,000 (adult population in 1993)
× 42.4% (percent of persons who have guns in their homes; obtained from GSS)
× 19% (percent of persons who were victims of criminal attacks; obtained from NCVS)
× 1.326% (percent of persons who defended themselves using a gun; obtained from Kleck and Gertz)
= 203,538 persons used guns defensively in 1993.

This estimate is slightly lower than the estimate that was obtained from the NCVS data. Hence, a better estimate of the true number of defensive firearm incidents that occurred in 1993 is between 203,000 and 226,000. Clearly, some of the assumptions made by Kleck and Gertz were not appropriate, and these assumptions greatly inflated their estimate of the number of persons who used firearms defensively. Finally, the Kleck and Gertz survey was conducted only in 1993. Hence, their data are over 20 years old.

Defensive gun use, as reported in the NCVS, was abnormally high in 1993. To get a better estimate of self-protective behaviors in the United States, we will now examine data from the 2014 NCVS. These are the most recent data available on self-protective behaviors. It is important to note that there were a large number of missing observations for the self-protective questions. In addition, for a single year, there are very few observations. Hence, please interpret the following results with caution.

In the 2014 NCVS, 10 respondents said that they fired a gun (attacked off) to defend themselves, and 18 said that they threatened the offender off with a gun. Assuming no double-counting, that is a total of 28 respondents who used a gun to defend themselves out of a total number of 1010 self-protective behaviors. Hence, according to the NCVS, in 2014, 2.8% of victims who engaged in a self-protective behavior used a gun. Although higher than the Kleck and Gertz estimate of 1.326%, the NCVS percentage only applies to those persons who were not only the victim but who also tried to defend themselves.

There are also questions in the NCVS on the effectiveness of the various self-protective behaviors. Unfortunately, the number of responses for those questions are extremely low and are not statistically significant. Hence, those data are not reported here.

Another report on defensive firearm use is the report "Firearm Violence, 1993–2011," which was prepared by the Bureau of Justice Statistics (Plant and Truman 2013). In this report, the following results, obtained from the NCVS for the years 2007–2011:

- About 43.8% of victims of violent crime offered no resistance.
- About 12% of property crime victims offered no resistance. (For 85.6% of property crimes, the victim was not present.)
- About 0.8% of violent crime victims used a gun to defend themselves.
- About 0.1% of property crime victims used a gun to defend themselves.
- Most victims used nonconfrontational tactics (running, yelling, and screaming).
- There were 338,700 incidents of defensive firearm use for the period 2007–2011. This translates into approximately 67,740 incidents per year.
- For the period 2007–2011, there were 114 million violent and property crimes.

Hence, based on these data defensive firearm use is not very common. Even the Kleck and Gertz study arrived at a very low value for the percentage of persons who used a gun defensively. The issue is more with how their percentage was applied.

In conclusion, defensive firearm use is considered by many gun rights activists to be one of the primary reasons for the Second Amendment. These activists believe that restrictions on the use of firearms result in law-abiding citizens being left unarmed and thus vulnerable to criminals. More innocent victims will die because they cannot defend themselves. They further believe that it is a constitutional right for a person to be allowed to defend themselves with a gun.

Unfortunately, the available data do not support this hypothesis. First, a minority of the population are victims of a criminal act in any given year. Even fewer are victims of violent crimes. The crime rate, or the percentage of persons who are victims of crime, is also much lower now than it has been for decades. Hence, the probability that an individual will be the victim of a crime is much lower now than it was 20 or 30 years ago.

Second, very few victims ever try to defend themselves using a gun. 56.2% of victims of violent crime attempt to defend themselves, but only 0.8% of them use a gun in self-defense. Hence, the importance of firearms in the area of self-defense is greatly overstated by gun rights activists. In addition, the data on the effectiveness of firearm self-protective behaviors are so inadequate that very little of statistical significance can be inferred from these data.

Third, the only other estimate of defensive firearm use comes from a study (Kleck and Gertz 1995) that is over 20 years old and has serious methodological issues, especially with regards to the way in which its estimate of defensive firearm use is applied. Whenever gun rights activists claim that there are over 2 million instances of defensive firearm use per year, they obtain this estimate from the Kleck and Gertz study.

Fourth, there is a serious need for much better data in this area. The NCVS must be expanded so that state-level analyses can be conducted. Without additional data, it is impossible to determine the effectiveness of castle doctrine and SYG laws on self-protective behaviors.

The NCVS questionnaire should be revised to allow for fewer open-ended questions and multiple responses. There should be direct questions regarding defensive firearm use. These questions should be asked of everybody, not just those who claim to be the victim of a crime. Further questioning could parse out responses that are inaccurate or responses that may indicate illegal activity.

Given the importance of defensive firearm use in the gun rights discussion, the issue of better data is not just an academic inquiry. It is also important that public policymakers have the necessary data to make informed decisions regarding the effectiveness and importance of defensive firearm use. If guns actually help victims defend themselves, then that would buttress the arguments that are made by gun rights activists, and it makes a strong case for fewer restrictions on guns. If, however, firearms are rarely used in self-defense, or if they are ineffective in such encounters, then defensive firearm use is one less argument that can be used by gun rights activists.

chapter four

Mass shootings in America

According to a recent report prepared by the Congressional Research Service (Bjelopera et al. 2013), a public mass shooting has four distinct attributes:

1. Occurred in a relatively public place.
2. Involved four or more deaths—not including the shooter.
3. Victims were selected randomly.
4. Shooting was not a means to a criminal end, such as robbery or terrorism.

Given this definition, many cases of multiple murders occur in the United States that would not be considered public mass shootings. There are, unfortunately, many examples of high-profile public mass shootings in the United States that fit this definition. It is important to note, however, that there are not as many public mass shootings as one would believe. Much of the data presented here were obtained from the website of *Mother Jones*, but they were corroborated with information from other sources as well (Follman et al. 2016). According to the *Mother Jones* website, there were only two mass shootings in 2014; nine people died in those incidents. In the same year, there were 11,961 total murders. Hence, these statistics illustrate the fact that mass shootings, although horrendous and very newsworthy, are also very rare. In addition, they are very random. In the past five years, mass shootings have occurred at schools, colleges, churches, temples, and restaurants. Many times, the shooter had no known motive. Many of the shooters committed suicide at the scene. The one common denominator of almost all of the mass shootings over the past 35 years is that they were, by and large, committed by men.

In addition, many of the perpetrators in these mass shootings used multiple types of firearms. Assault rifles were not the predominant type of weapon used in mass shootings. Handguns were the most commonly used type of firearm in mass shootings (32.99% of mass shootings); rifles (assault weapons are a type of rifle) were used in only 8.25% of mass shootings (Huff-Corzine et al. 2013). Hence, the typical mass shooter is male, uses a handgun, and commits his crime in a public place where people congregate. Beyond that, there is very little that connects the various mass shootings that have occurred over the years. Table 4.1 lists all the public mass shootings since 1982. This table was obtained from the *Mother Jones* website (Follman et al. 2016).

As can be ascertained from Table 4.1, there were very few mass shootings during the 1980s, but their frequency has increased significantly since then. There were only 8 mass shootings during the period 1982–1989, but there were 23 during the period 1990–1999, 20 during the period 2000–2009, and 22 during the period 2010–2015. This increase in the frequency of mass shootings is even more interesting because, in the 1980s, there were no federal background checks, and there was no assault weapons ban. In fact, during the period of the Assault Weapons Ban, and after the Brady Bill came into effect (1994–2004), there were 17 mass shooting incidents, including the shooting at Columbine High School in Littleton, Colorado. Hence, stricter gun control measures appear to have had little effect on the number of mass shootings.

Unfortunately, very little research has been conducted on the relationship between gun control and mass shootings. One of the primary reasons for this lack of research is the paucity of data on mass shootings. During most years, less than 10 mass shootings occur nationwide. Hence, from a statistical standpoint, the population of mass shootings is too small to determine the relationships between gun control laws and mass shootings.

One of the most recent research studies on this topic is Gius (2015a). The purpose of this study was to determine the effects of federal and state assault weapons bans on public mass shootings. Using a Poisson effects model and data for the period 1982–2011, it was found that both state and federal assault weapons bans had statistically significant and negative effects on mass shooting fatalities but that only the federal Assault Weapons Ban had a negative effect on mass shooting injuries. One possible reason for this result is that assault weapons have much higher rates of fire than conventional, nonsemiautomatic weapons. Hence, the perpetrator is able to fire more rounds, thus potentially resulting in more injuries and deaths.

Chapman et al. (2006) examined the effects of Australia's 1996 gun law reforms on firearm-related homicides, including mass shootings, and found that, after the enactment of the laws, there were declines in firearm-related homicides and suicides but no significant decrease in unintentional firearm deaths. It was also noted that there were 13 mass shooting incidents in Australia in the 18 years prior to the enactment of the stricter gun control measures but no mass shootings since the passage of the laws.

Table 4.1 Mass shootings

Location	Year	Fatalities	Injured
Orlando, FL	2016	49	53
Hesston, KS	2016	3	14
Kalamazoo, County, MI	2016	6	2
San Bernardino, CA	2015	14	21
Roseburg, OR	2015	9	9
Chattanooga, TN	2015	5	2
Charleston, SC	2015	9	1
Marysville, WA	2014	5	1
Alturas, CA	2014	4	2
Washington, DC	2013	13	8
Hialeah, FL	2013	7	0
Santa Monica, CA	2013	6	3
Federal Way, WA	2013	5	0
Herkimer County, NY	2013	5	2
Newtown, CT	2012	28	2
Minneapolis, MN	2012	7	1
Oak Creek, WI	2012	7	3
Aurora, CO	2012	12	58
Seattle, WA	2012	6	1
Oakland, CA	2012	7	3
Norcross, GA	2012	5	0
Seal Beach, CA	2011	8	1
Carson City, NV	2011	5	7
Tucson, AZ	2011	6	13
Manchester, CT	2010	9	2
Parkland, WA	2009	4	1
Fort Hood, TX	2009	13	30
Binghamton, NY	2009	14	4
Carthage, NC	2009	8	3
Henderson, KY	2008	6	1
DeKalb, IL	2008	6	21
Kirkwood, MO	2008	6	2
Omaha, NE	2007	9	4
Crandon, WI	2007	6	1
Blacksburg, VA	2007	33	23
Salt Lake City, UT	2007	6	4
Lancaster County, PA	2006	6	5

(Continued)

Table 4.1 (Continued) Mass shootings

Location	Year	Fatalities	Injured
Seattle, WA	2006	7	2
Goleta, CA	2006	8	0
Red Lake, MN	2005	10	5
Brookfield, WI	2005	7	4
Columbus, OH	2004	5	7
Meridian, MS	2003	7	8
Melrose Park, IL	2001	5	4
Wakefield, MA	2000	7	0
Tampa, FL	1999	5	3
Honolulu, HI	1999	7	0
Fort Worth, TX	1999	8	7
Atlanta, GA	1999	9	13
Littleton, CO	1999	15	24
Springfield, OR	1998	4	25
Jonesboro, AR	1998	5	10
Newington, CT	1998	5	1
Orange, CA	1997	5	2
Aiken, SC	1997	4	3
Fort Lauderdale, FL	1996	6	1
Corpus Christi, TX	1995	6	0
Fairchild Air Force Base, WA	1994	5	23
Aurora, CO	1993	4	1
Garden City, NY	1993	6	19
Fayetteville, NC	1993	4	8
San Francisco, CA	1993	9	6
Watkins Glen, NY	1992	5	0
Olivehurst, CA	1992	4	10
Royal Oak, MI	1991	5	5
Iowa City, IA	1991	6	1
Killeen, TX	1991	24	20
Jacksonville, FL	1990	10	4
Louisville, KY	1989	9	12
Stockton, CA	1989	6	29
Sunnyvale, CA	1988	7	4
Palm Bay, FL	1987	6	14
Edmond, OK	1986	15	6

(*Continued*)

Table 4.1 (Continued) Mass shootings

Location	Year	Fatalities	Injured
San Ysidro, CA	1984	22	19
Dallas, TX	1984	6	1
Miami, FL	1982	8	3

Source: Follman, Mark et al., A guide to mass shootings in America., *Mother Jones,* 2012, http://www.motherjones.com/politics/2012/07/mass-shootings -map. February 1, 2016.

Duwe et al. (2002) examined the effects of right-to-carry laws on mass shootings. Using data for the period 1977–1999, the authors employed both Poisson and negative binomial models and found that right-to-carry laws had no statistically significant effects on mass shootings. Finally, Lott and Landes (2000) looked at mass shooting incidents also for the period 1977–1997 and found that states that enacted right-to-carry laws had fewer mass shootings than states that did not enact such laws. It is important to note, however, that during most of the period examined by Lott and Landes, there were very few mass shootings.

Hence, the results of research on the effects of gun control on mass shootings are mixed. Gius (2015a) found that assault weapons bans reduced the fatalities and injuries resulting from mass shootings, while Lott and Landes (2000) found that permissive concealed carry laws resulted in fewer mass shootings. Given the very small number of mass shootings committed in a given year, these mixed results are not unexpected.

Regarding policy proposals that can be derived from this research, unfortunately, there is no policy that can prevent random events as mass shootings. Given that they occur at such a multitude of different places, and given that the motives behind these shootings are typically unknown, it is very difficult to prevent such shootings. In addition, as was noted previously, although assault weapons are used in many of the high-profile shootings, they are not the primary weapon that is used in mass shootings. Instead, handguns are the primary weapon. One could possibly argue that if the supply of weapons was severely curtailed, then all gun-related murders, including mass shootings, would decline.

chapter five

Suicides and accidental firearm deaths in America

In 2014, there were 42,773 suicides and 136,053 unintentional (accidental) deaths. Of these, 21,334 suicides and 586 unintentional deaths were firearm related. In addition, whereas firearm suicide rates, have been increasing since 1999, firearm accidental death rates have fallen over the same period. Please see Tables 5.1 through 5.8 for more detailed information. All data presented in these tables have been obtained from the Centers for Disease Control and Prevention's (CDC's) Fatal Injury Reports.

As can be ascertained from these tables, for the year 2014, 50% of all suicides were firearm related, whereas only 0.43% of unintentional deaths were firearm related. For youths, 41% of suicides were firearm related, but only 1.4% of unintentional deaths were due to firearms. These data suggest that, although firearms are used very frequently in suicides, they are not a very significant factor in accidental deaths.

In order to more fully illustrate the extent and prevalence of suicide and firearm-related suicide, Table 5.9 presents the state-level data on suicides for 2014. Given the rarity of firearm-related unintentional deaths state-level data are not available for this type of fatal injury.

Montana had the highest overall suicide rate and the largest percentage of suicides that were committed using a gun. New York and the District of Columbia had the lowest overall suicide rates. Hawaii had the smallest percentage of suicides that were committed using a firearm. Although the data presented here are purely descriptive and do not imply causality, it appears as if states with less restrictive gun control laws had larger percentages of suicides that were committed using a gun. States with very restrictive gun control laws, such as California, Connecticut, Hawaii, Illinois, and New York, had firearm suicide percentages below 40%. Although no causation is implied by these statistics, there appears to be a relationship between gun control and firearm suicide rates.

Regarding some of the more relevant research on guns and suicide, Lester and Murrell (1982) examined the effects of gun control laws on state-level suicide rates. Looking at data from 1960 and 1970, a principal component analysis was used to determine the correlation between gun control laws and suicide rates. The results of the study suggested that

Table 5.1 Total suicides

Year	Deaths	Rate (per 100,000 persons)
1999	29,199	10.46
2000	29,350	10.43
2001	30,622	10.75
2002	31,655	11.01
2003	31,484	10.85
2004	32,439	11.08
2005	32,637	11.04
2006	33,300	11.16
2007	34,598	11.49
2008	36,035	11.85
2009	36,909	12.03
2010	38,364	12.43
2011	39,518	12.68
2012	40,600	12.93
2013	41,149	13
2014	42,773	13.41

Source: Fatal Injury Reports, Centers for Disease Control and Prevention, National Center for Injury Prevention and Control: Washington, DC.

Table 5.2 Total unintentional deaths

Year	Deaths	Rate (per 100,000 persons)
1999	97,860	35.07
2000	97,900	34.79
2001	101,537	35.63
2002	106,742	37.11
2003	109,277	37.67
2004	112,012	38.25
2005	117,809	39.87
2006	121,599	40.75
2007	123,706	41.07
2008	121,902	40.09
2009	118,021	38.47
2010	120,859	39.15
2011	126,438	40.56
2012	127,792	40.68
2013	130,557	41.25
2014	136,053	42.67

Source: Fatal Injury Reports, Centers for Disease Control and Prevention, National Center for Injury Prevention and Control: Washington, DC.

Table 5.3 Firearm suicides

Year	Deaths	Rate (per 100,000 persons)
1999	16,599	5.95
2000	16,586	5.89
2001	16,869	5.92
2002	17,108	5.95
2003	16,907	5.83
2004	16,750	5.72
2005	17,002	5.75
2006	16,883	5.66
2007	17,352	5.76
2008	18,223	5.99
2009	18,735	6.11
2010	19,392	6.28
2011	19,990	6.41
2012	20,666	6.58
2013	21,175	6.69
2014	21,334	6.69

Source: *Fatal Injury Reports,* Centers for Disease Control and Prevention, National Center for Injury Prevention and Control: Washington, DC.

Table 5.4 Unintentional firearm deaths

Year	Deaths	Rate (per 100,000 persons)
1999	824	0.3
2000	776	0.28
2001	802	0.28
2002	762	0.26
2003	730	0.25
2004	649	0.22
2005	789	0.27
2006	642	0.22
2007	613	0.2
2008	592	0.19
2009	554	0.18
2010	606	0.2
2011	591	0.19
2012	548	0.17
2013	505	0.16
2014	586	0.18

Source: *Fatal Injury Reports,* Centers for Disease Control and Prevention, National Center for Injury Prevention and Control: Washington, DC.

Table 5.5 Youth suicides, ages 0–18

Year	Deaths	Rate (per 100,000 persons)
1999	1415	1.86
2000	1493	1.96
2001	1400	1.82
2002	1331	1.73
2003	1285	1.66
2004	1471	1.9
2005	1408	1.81
2006	1296	1.66
2007	1231	1.57
2008	1344	1.71
2009	1467	1.86
2010	1456	1.85
2011	1568	2
2012	1590	2.04
2013	1645	2.11
2014	1785	2.29

Source: *Fatal Injury Reports*, Centers for Disease Control and Prevention, National Center for Injury Prevention and Control: Washington, DC.

Table 5.6 Youth firearm suicides, ages 0–18

Year	Deaths	Rate (per 100,000 persons)
1999	809	1.07
2000	754	0.99
2001	656	0.85
2002	603	0.78
2003	568	0.73
2004	595	0.77
2005	600	0.77
2006	535	0.69
2007	493	0.63
2008	529	0.67
2009	589	0.75
2010	556	0.71
2011	633	0.81
2012	636	0.81
2013	668	0.86
2014	732	0.94

Source: *Fatal Injury Reports*, Centers for Disease Control and Prevention, National Center for Injury Prevention and Control: Washington, DC.

Table 5.7 Youth unintentional deaths, ages 0–18

Year	Deaths	Rate (per 100,000 persons)
1999	10,799	14.22
2000	10,659	13.96
2001	10,377	13.52
2002	10,524	13.66
2003	10,216	13.22
2004	10,391	13.41
2005	9939	12.78
2006	9791	12.54
2007	9715	12.39
2008	8523	10.83
2009	7712	9.8
2010	7300	9.28
2011	7076	9.03
2012	6823	8.74
2013	6455	8.29
2014	6347	8.16

Source: *Fatal Injury Reports,* Centers for Disease Control and Prevention, National Center for Injury Prevention and Control: Washington, DC.

Table 5.8 Youth firearm unintentional deaths, ages 0–18

Year	Deaths	Rate (per 100,000 persons)
1999	189	0.25
2000	174	0.23
2001	154	0.2
2002	143	0.19
2003	127	0.16
2004	121	0.16
2005	154	0.2
2006	125	0.16
2007	122	0.16
2008	110	0.14
2009	96	0.12
2010	114	0.14
2011	122	0.16
2012	94	0.12
2013	108	0.14
2014	89	0.11

Source: *Fatal Injury Reports,* Centers for Disease Control and Prevention, National Center for Injury Prevention and Control: Washington, DC.

Table 5.9 State-level suicides, 2014

State	Suicides	Rate	Firearm suicides	Rate	Percent of firearm
Alabama	715	14.74	479	9.88	67%
Alaska	167	22.67	115	15.61	69%
Arizona	1244	18.48	683	10.15	55%
Arkansas	515	17.36	323	10.89	63%
California	4214	10.86	1582	4.08	38%
Colorado	1083	20.22	539	10.06	50%
Connecticut	379	10.54	125	3.48	33%
Delaware	126	13.47	59	6.31	47%
District of Columbia	52	7.89	14	2.12	27%
Florida	3035	15.26	1538	7.73	51%
Georgia	1294	12.82	840	8.32	65%
Hawaii	204	14.37	33	2.32	16%
Idaho	320	19.58	182	11.14	59%
Illinois	1398	10.85	533	4.14	38%
Indiana	948	14.37	528	8	57%
Iowa	407	13.1	194	6.24	48%
Kansas	455	15.67	238	8.2	52%
Kentucky	727	16.47	469	10.63	65%
Louisiana	679	14.6	444	9.55	65%
Maine	220	16.54	116	8.72	53%
Maryland	606	10.14	277	4.63	46%
Massachusetts	596	8.84	130	1.93	22%
Michigan	1354	13.66	671	6.77	50%
Minnesota	686	12.57	308	5.64	49%
Mississippi	380	12.69	251	8.38	66%
Missouri	1017	16.77	588	9.7	58%
Montana	251	24.52	149	14.56	59%
Nebraska	251	13.34	133	7.07	53%
Nevada	573	20.18	309	10.88	54%
New Hampshire	247	18.62	110	8.29	45%
New Jersey	786	8.79	194	2.17	25%
New Mexico	449	21.53	244	11.7	54%
New York	1700	8.61	474	2.4	28%
North Carolina	1351	13.59	759	7.63	56%

(Continued)

Table 5.9 (Continued) State-level suicides, 2014

State	Suicides	Rate	Firearm suicides	Rate	Percent of firearm
North Dakota	137	18.53	85	11.49	62%
Ohio	1491	12.86	744	6.42	50%
Oklahoma	736	18.98	435	11.22	59%
Oregon	782	19.7	422	10.63	54%
Pennsylvania	1817	14.21	897	7.01	49%
Rhode Island	113	10.71	20	1.9	18%
South Carolina	753	15.58	479	9.91	64%
South Dakota	141	16.53	76	8.91	54%
Tennessee	948	14.47	596	9.1	63%
Texas	3254	12.07	1789	6.64	55%
Utah	559	18.99	278	9.45	50%
Vermont	124	19.79	59	9.42	48%
Virginia	1122	13.48	625	7.51	56%
Washington	1119	15.85	551	7.8	49%
West Virginia	359	19.4	217	11.73	60%
Wisconsin	769	13.36	352	6.11	46%
Wyoming	120	20.54	78	13.35	65%

Source: Fatal Injury Reports, Centers for Disease Control and Prevention, National Center for Injury Prevention and Control: Washington, DC.

states with stricter gun control laws had lower suicide rates; however, these states also had higher suicide rates by means other than firearms. This result indicates that suicide victims may be using alternative methods when obtaining a firearm becomes difficult.

Sommers (1984) looked at state-level data for 1970 and attempted to determine the effects of several gun control laws on suicide rates. Estimating suicide rates by both race and sex, the author found that most gun control measures were negatively related to suicide. Of all the equations that he estimated, the one that had the most statistically significant gun control variables was the female regression. This is an interesting result since most suicides by firearm are committed by men and not women.

Lester (1988), in an attempt to corroborate the findings of his 1982 study, looked at not only gun control laws but also gun ownership rates. The author used estimated regional gun ownership rates. His results suggested that gun control laws were not significantly related to suicide rates but that gun ownership rates were related to suicide rates. He concluded that limiting the availability of firearms may reduce suicide rates.

Yang and Lester (1991) attempted to correct some perceived shortcomings in Sommers' 1984 study and tried to determine if suicide rates by means other than firearms increased in states with restrictive gun control laws. Using a model very similar to that employed by Sommers (1984), the authors estimated the equations for the total suicide rate and for various types of suicide (i.e., by firearm, by jumping, etc.). Their results indicated that gun control was significant and negative for both total suicide and firearm suicide. For jumping suicide, gun control had a positive effect. For all other types of suicide, gun control was insignificant. According to the authors, these results suggested that gun control does not make suicide victims switch to another type of suicide. Yang and Lester concluded that gun control laws are significant deterrents to suicide.

Marvell (2001) looked at the effects of the federal Violent Crime Control and Law Enforcement Act of 1994 on homicides and suicides. This act banned the possession of handguns by persons under 18 years of age. The authors looked at the effects of this law on both juvenile and overall homicide (1979–1998) and suicide (1976–1999) rates. Using state-level data, Marvell found that federal and state laws on the underage possession of handguns had no statistically significant effects on youth suicide rates.

Duggan (2003) examined the correlation between gun ownership and suicide rates. His primary objective was to determine if the direction of causation is from guns to suicides or from suicides to guns. Using estimated gun ownership rates, he found that states with higher suicide rates had higher gun ownership rates. However, he noted that a significant part of this relationship between gun availability and suicides can be explained by the correlation between guns and suicidal tendencies. Duggan believed that a primary reason why most prior studies found positive relationships between guns and suicide is that individuals who own guns are more likely to have suicidal tendencies. Finally, the author found that while both gun ownership and suicide rates have declined over a 20-year period, the decline in gun ownership cannot explain a significant part of the decline in suicides during the same period. It is important to note, however, that Duggan did not use any other explanatory variables aside from gun ownership rates, and his R^2s were all less than 10%.

Conner and Zhong (2003) used a methodology similar to that employed by Lester and Murrell (1982) and attempted to determine if more restrictive gun control laws resulted in lower suicide rates. The authors categorized states based upon the presence of various gun control measures, such as licensing and registration, background checks, minimum age requirements, waiting periods, restrictions on assault weapons, safe storage requirements, and various other laws. Using state-level data, the authors found that states that had more restrictive gun control laws had lower overall suicide rates.

Gius (2011) looked at the effects of various gun control measures and gun ownership rates on firearm- and non-firearm-related suicide rates. Using state-level data for the years 1995–2004 and looking at only three gun control measures: (1) permits for handguns, (2) registration of handguns, and (3) waiting periods for handgun purchases, the author found that only the permit requirement had a statistically significant and negative effect on firearm-related suicides but that the registration requirement actually increased non-firearm-related suicides. Hence, the author concluded that suicide victims may be switching methods due to gun control measures.

Finally, Lang (2013) used state-level data on background checks as a proxy for gun availability. His primary explanatory variable was the number of background checks in a state, and the dependent variable was the change in the suicide rate. Control variables include the unemployment rate, the number of per-capita bankruptcies, the percentage of people who are uninsured, the percentage of persons under 18, and the percentage of persons older than 65. Using a fixed-effects model, the author found that the overall suicide rate and the non-firearm suicide rate were not significantly related to background checks. However, an increase in firearm background checks resulted in an increase in the firearm suicide rate. Lang (2013) is one of the few studies that found that an increase in the restrictiveness of a gun control measure resulted in an increase in firearm suicides.

Regarding research on firearm-related unintentional deaths, one of the first studies on this topic was Lester and Murrell (1981). The authors used an index of gun control laws and attempted to determine if there was any correlation between stricter gun control laws and firearm-related unintentional death rates. Using only a simple correlation analysis, Lester and Murrell (1981) found that states with stricter gun control laws not only had lower rates of firearm-related unintentional deaths but also had lower unintentional death rates due to poisoning and drowning, two factors that could not possibly be affected by gun control laws.

Lester (1993) looked at the availability of guns and the incidence of firearm-related unintentional death rates. Using a questionable measure of firearm availability (the percentages of suicides and homicides involving a gun), the author found a positive correlation between gun availability and firearm-related unintentional death rates. Unfortunately, this article suffers from various shortcomings, including a questionable measure of gun availability, reliance on a very simple correlation analysis, and looking at 17 nations for only one year (1980).

Leenaars and Lester (1997) examined the effects of gun control on firearm-related unintentional deaths in Canada. Using data for the period 1969–1985 and using only a very simple regression analysis (only three explanatory variables were used, including the gun control law), the authors found that the Criminal Law Amendment of 1977 resulted in lower rates of firearm-related unintentional deaths for both men and women.

Lott and Whitley (2001) examined the effects of safe-storage laws on juvenile firearm-related suicides and unintentional deaths. The authors looked at child access prevention (CAP) laws and laws requiring some type of gun lock to be used to secure a firearm. State-level data for the period 1977–1996 were used. The authors used a fixed-effects Tobit model that included as explanatory variables a safe-storage dummy variable, non-firearm unintentional death rates, adult firearm unintentional death rates, and various control variables. Lott and Whitley found that safe storage had no significant effects on youth firearm-related unintentional deaths or suicides.

Finally, one of the most recent papers in this area examined the determinants of both suicides and unintentional deaths. Gius (2015b) looked at the effects of CAP laws and minimum age laws on youth firearm-related suicide and unintentional death rates. CAP laws impose criminal liabilities on adults who allow children to have unsupervised access to firearms. Although there is no federal CAP law, many states have enacted such laws. As of 2010, 16 states have enacted some type of CAP law. In addition to CAP laws, many states also have laws requiring minimum ages to possess firearms, especially handguns. Some states also have minimum age requirements for the possession of long guns (rifles and shotguns); the federal government has no long gun possession minimum age requirement. There are, of course, exceptions to these laws, including hunting, target practice, and other legitimate activities. In addition to these state regulations, federal law prohibits the possession of handguns by any person under the age of 18. In order to determine if these laws have any significant effects on youth suicides or unintentional deaths, a fixed-effects regression model, controlling for both state-level and year-specific effects, was used. Results suggested that state-level minimum age laws have no significant effects on either youth suicides or unintentional deaths and that state-level CAP laws have no significant effects on unintentional deaths. States with CAP laws, however, have lower rates of youth suicide, and, after the enactment of the federal minimum age requirement, both youth suicide and unintentional death rates fell.

Evidence from research in this area suggests that gun control laws may have significant and negative effects on suicides and accidental deaths. Unfortunately, many prior studies used indices of gun control in their estimation of the determinants of suicides and unintentional deaths, thus making it difficult to determine which specific gun control measures may actually reduce suicides and unintentional deaths. In addition, many prior studies looked at the effects of various measures of gun availability or gun prevalence on suicides and accidental deaths and not gun control measures. Hence, given the mixed results and the methodology of research in this area, it is difficult to determine which gun control laws would have the most pronounced effects on suicides and unintentional deaths. Although some studies have found that minimum age requirements and CAP laws may reduce firearm suicides and unintentional deaths, the evidence is not overwhelming. This is an extremely important topic primarily because there are twice as many firearm suicides as there are firearm murders. Hence, more research is warranted in this area.

chapter six

Gun control in America

There were no federal laws and few state laws regulating the ownership of firearms prior to the 1930s. In looking at federal regulations, the first federal gun control law was the National Firearms Act (NFA) of 1934. The NFA was enacted in response to increasing crime brought on by Prohibition; its primary purpose was to reduce the supply of very dangerous and very concealable weapons, such as machine guns (Tommy guns), sawed-off shotguns, and silencers.

The next major federal gun control law was the Federal Firearms Act (FFA) of 1938. This law created the federal firearms license (FFL) for firearm dealers. Only individuals who sold relatively *large* quantities of firearms in a given year were required to obtain an FFL. This law also required FFL dealers to keep written records of firearm transactions, and dealers could not sell weapons to persons who were convicted felons or who were prohibited in some other way from owning a firearm. This law was repealed by the Gun Control Act (GCA) of 1968.

After the FFA, there were no new federal gun control laws until the GCA was enacted. The impetus for this law was the assassination of President John F. Kennedy. The original bill languished in committee for several years until the assassinations of Robert Kennedy and Martin Luther King, Jr. in 1968 renewed efforts to enact a new, stricter federal gun control law. Finally, in October of 1968, the GCA was signed into law by President Lyndon B. Johnson. Although this law repealed the FFA, the GCA retained many of the components of the FFA, including the creation of FFL dealers and the requirement that certain prohibited persons were not allowed to own guns. In addition, the GCA prohibited the mail order sales of firearms (President Kennedy was assassinated by a rifle that was purchased through the mail) and required all firearms manufactured and sold in the United States to have a serial number engraved on them. It is a felony to deface the serial number, but guns manufactured prior to 1968 were exempt from this requirement.

Although there were several federal gun control laws that were enacted in the years following the passage of the GCA (the most notable was the creation of the Bureau of Alcohol, Tobacco, and Firearms in 1972), the next major federal law was the Brady Handgun Violence Prevention Act (Brady Act) in 1993. This law mandated a five-day waiting period for handgun purchases during which time a criminal background check would be conducted. This law also required that, by 1998, a National Instant Criminal Background Check System (NICS) would be created, and the act's provisions would be extended to purchasers of long guns and to persons who redeem pawned firearms.

The following year, the Violent Crime Control and Law Enforcement Act (the Assault Weapons Ban) was passed. Among other things, this law banned the manufacture of certain types of semiautomatic assault weapons. This law expired in 2004. Since the passage of the Assault Weapons Ban in 1994, there have been no new federal gun control laws.

As can be ascertained from the above discussion, there are relatively few federal gun control laws. All of the federal laws deal with firearm transfers, and, even with regards to transfers, only sales by FFL dealers are regulated by the federal government. Private sales are unregulated at the federal level. There are no federal laws regulating the concealed or open carry of firearms, and the only firearms that are banned at the federal level are machine guns.

Most of the restrictive gun control laws are at the state level. There are state laws that ban assault weapons, require the registration of certain firearms, and mandate permits to purchase firearms. It is important to note, however, that most states have few restrictions on firearm ownership. For years, Vermont has had the distinction of being the state with the fewest restrictions on gun ownership. Given that background checks are conducted through the NICS, most background checks are completed within a few minutes. In most states, if a person buys a gun from a private party, then no background check is required. In many states, no permit is required for open or concealed carry of firearms.

A detailed explanation of some of the most common state- and federal-level gun control measures and a description of the relevant research on these laws follow. Only those gun control laws that have been the subject of recent academic research regarding their effects on crime or violent deaths are examined. There are other state-level gun control laws, such as waiting periods and multiple gun sale restrictions, that are not examined because so few states have these types of laws.

Assault weapons

Very few murders are committed using assault weapons. Although the Federal Bureau of Investigation (FBI) does not collect data on the number of murders committed using an assault weapon, data are collected on the number of murders committed using a long gun; an assault weapon is a type of long gun. In 2014, only 248 murders were committed using a long gun, 8124 murders were committed using any type of firearm,

11,961 murders in total were committed that year. If all murders committed using long guns could have been avoided, total murders would have fallen by only 2%. Hence, even though many of the murders committed with assault weapons are very tragic (Newtown, Connecticut; San Bernardino, California), relatively few murders are committed using an assault weapon. That is why most research has found that assault weapons bans have little-to-no effect on the overall murder rate.

At the federal level, certain assault weapons were banned during the period 1994–2004. The Violent Crime Control and Law Enforcement Act of 1994 outlawed semiautomatic weapons (weapons that fire one shot each time that the trigger is pulled) that had certain distinguishing features, such as pistol grips, flash hiders, and folding stocks (Koper 2004). The possession of machine guns, which are guns that fire continuously when the trigger is pulled, have been heavily regulated at the federal level for decades. In addition to banning certain types of guns, the 1994 law also prohibited large-capacity magazines that held more than 10 rounds of ammunition. This prohibition affected many more types of guns than the assault weapons ban did primarily because many semiautomatic weapons, including handguns, were capable of using large-capacity magazines.

The 1994 law had several loopholes and exemptions. One such exemption was that all assault weapons and large-capacity magazines manufactured prior to the effective date of the ban were legal to own and transfer. It would have taken years for these assault weapons to malfunction and wear down, and only then would the ban have had any lasting impact on the overall supply of assault weapons and large-capacity magazines.

Another weakness in the 1994 law was that only exact copies of banned assault weapons were also banned. Hence, many gun manufacturers made a few cosmetic changes to their *banned* weapons and turned them into legal weapons. Modifications, such as the removal of a flash suppressor or pistol grip, would turn a previously banned weapon into a legal weapon, even though the rate of fire remained the same. In addition, there was no prohibition against new, legal assault weapons being able to accept older, grandfathered large-capacity magazines. Most legal assault weapons produced during the ban years (1994–2004) could easily accommodate preban large-capacity magazines. Hence, in the short run, the effect of the 1994 law on the supply of assault weapons and large-capacity magazines was minimal at best. The federal assault weapons ban expired in 2004.

In looking at the history of state-level assault weapons bans, no state had a ban before 1989. California was the first state to enact such a law. Currently, only seven states and the District of Columbia have some type of assault weapons ban. Those seven states are as follows: (1) California, (2) Connecticut, (3) Hawaii, (4) Maryland, (5) Massachusetts, (6) New Jersey, and (7) New York. Most of these states allow assault weapons that were owned prior to their bans, although they usually require a permit to own an assault weapon. Hawaii only bans assault pistols.

Research on assault weapons bans is very limited. One of the few studies that examined assault weapons bans was Koper and Roth (2001). They looked at the effects of the 1994 federal assault weapon ban on violent crimes. Using state-level data from 1970 to 1995, the authors found that the federal ban had little-to-no effect on homicide rates. One possible reason for these results is that the ban was in effect for only one year when their study was conducted.

In Koper (2004), it was concluded that the federal assault weapons ban had minimal effects on gun-related violence. Koper (2004) found that reducing the supply of assault weapons and large-capacity magazines may have had *nontrivial* effects on gunshot victims. Given that assault weapons fire many more rounds per minute than other types of firearms, attacks with assault weapons usually result in more shots fired and potentially more victims than attacks with other types of weapons (Koper 2004). Koper's limited conclusions suggest that any effect that the ban may have had on violent crime was probably minimal at best, but if the ban had been extended, then that effect would have increased in magnitude but still would have been negligible.

Gius (2014) attempted to determine the effects of state-level assault weapons bans and concealed weapons laws on state-level murder rates. Using data for the period 1980–2009 and controlling for state and year fixed effects, his results suggested that state-level assault weapons bans did not significantly affect murder rates. In addition, it was found that the effect of the federal assault weapons ban was significant and positive. Murder rates were 19.3% higher when the federal ban was in effect.

Given the evidence from available research, it appears as if assault weapons bans are not effective in reducing the gun-related murder rate. This result is not unexpected, especially given that rifles are used in few murders and other violent crimes. Hence, even though assault weapons are used in many high-profile murders and mass shootings, the reality is that they are too large and too cumbersome to use in typical murder scenarios. Therefore, given the research, assault weapons bans are rather ineffective in reducing gun-related crime.

Background checks

Starting in February of 1994, the federal government required all buyers of handguns to undergo a background check in order to determine if they are legally allowed to possess a gun. Prior to that year, there was no federal requirement for criminal background checks for firearm purchasers. This requirement was part of the Brady Handgun Violence Prevention Act

(Brady Act) of 1993. The potential reasons why a person may be prohibited from owning a firearm include felony convictions, felony indictments, domestic violence misdemeanors, restraining orders, fugitive status, illegal alien status, mental illness or disability, drug addiction, and local or state prohibition. From February of 1994 to November of 1998, the act only applied to handgun sales. In November of 1998, the permanent provisions of the Brady Act took effect. These permanent provisions established the NICS and extended the act's provisions to purchasers of long guns and to persons who redeem pawned firearms. States have the option of conducting their own background checks (point of contact [PoC]), or they may have the checks performed by the FBI.

The procedure for conducting a firearms background check is initiated by an FFL dealer. The prospective purchaser of a gun must complete a federal Firearms Transaction Record and must provide a government-issued photo identification card. The FFL dealer then contacts the FBI or state PoC in order to determine if the prospective buyer is legally allowed to purchase a firearm. The FFL dealer is then notified whether or not the sale may proceed or if the sale must be delayed pending further investigation. If the FFL dealer has not been notified within three business days, the sale may be completed; this type of sale is known as a default proceed. From 1994 to 2009, only 1.8% of firearm sales were denied.

Under the Brady Act, sales conducted through unlicensed firearms dealers (private sales) do not require background checks. Some states, however, require background checks for all purchasers of firearms, even if the transaction is conducted privately.

Finally, a person holding a state-issued firearms permit is exempt from background checks for a period of five years after the issuance of the permit; this exemption even applies to sales that are conducted through an FFL dealer. Given the aforementioned loopholes and exemptions, a sizeable percentage of firearm purchases are not conditional upon a background check.

The following states require that some or all private transfers of firearms be subject to a background check:

- California
- Colorado
- Connecticut
- Delaware
- District of Columbia
- Hawaii
- Illinois
- Iowa (handguns only)
- Maryland (handguns only)

- Massachusetts
- Michigan (handguns only)
- Nebraska (handguns only)
- New Jersey
- New York
- North Carolina (handguns only)
- Oregon
- Pennsylvania (handguns only)
- Rhode Island
- Washington

Hence, most states require no additional criminal background check beyond that required by federal law.

Regarding research in this area, the general assumption is that by keeping guns out of the hands of dangerous persons, gun-related crime should fall. Unfortunately, given that private sales in most of the country are not subject to background checks, the impact of background checks may be somewhat muted. The precise number of firearm sales conducted without a background check is unknown. In a 1997 study published by the National Institute of Justice, Cook and Ludwig estimated that 60% of gun sales involved an FFL dealer and thus were subject to a criminal background check. They further estimated that about 2 million firearm transfers per year were private. Unfortunately, this is the only study that attempted to estimate the number of firearms sold without a background check. Given that the study is almost 20 years old, and given that several laws regarding background checks have taken effect since then, it is highly unlikely that 40% of firearm transfers in 2015 were conducted without a background check. Hence, we do not know how many guns are sold or exchanged without some form of background check in the United States.

Research on background checks and their impact on crime is somewhat limited. One of the earliest studies on this topic was Ludwig and Cook (2000). Looking at state-level data for the years 1985–1997, the authors found that the Brady Act did not have statistically significant effects on homicide or the overall suicide rates. However, they did find that the Brady Act was negatively related to the firearm suicide rate for persons aged 55 and older. Given this limited finding, the authors concluded that the Brady Act was not very effective in reducing gun-related violence. It is important to note, however, that this study only looked at the effects of the Brady Act on homicides and suicides; it did not examine the effects of state-mandated background checks on these crimes. In addition, most of the years examined in this study were prior to the enactment of the Brady

Act. Finally, this is the only study on this topic that found that background checks were not significantly related to homicides or murder.

Studies that found that background checks were negatively related to murder include Ruddell and Mays (2005), Sumner et al. (2008), Sen and Panjamapirom (2012), Fleegler et al. (2013), and Webster et al. (2013, 2014). All of these studies looked at the effects of state background checks on gun-related murders or other gun-related fatalities. All used state-level data. All of these studies found that states that conducted more thorough and extensive background checks had fewer gun-related murders. Although there were some issues with these studies (the use of questionable indices for measuring the strictness of background checks, small sample sizes), overall, they found that stricter and more universal background checks reduce firearm murders and suicides.

The most recent study that examined the effects of background checks on crime is Gius (2015c). The purpose of this study was to determine if firearm background checks are significantly related to gun-related murder rates. This study differs from prior research in several ways. First, a large longitudinal data set was used; data for 50 states for the period 1980–2011 were examined. Second, the effects of both federal and state background checks, including state-mandated private sales background checks, were estimated. Finally, a fixed-effects model that controls for both state-level and year-specific effects was used. The results of this study suggested that states that require dealer background checks have lower gun-related murder rates than other states. In addition, after the implementation of the Brady Act, gun-related murder rates fell. However, the results also suggest that, for the entire period in question, states with private sales background checks had higher gun-related murder rates than states with no such background checks. If one only looks at the Brady Act period, however, then the private sales background check variable is insignificant.

One possible reason for the results found in Gius (2015c) is the fact that very few states conduct universal background checks. In addition, given that, in most states, no background check is required for private sales, many persons, especially those with criminal intent, can easily travel to a state with no background check requirement to purchase a firearm.

Most of the research in this area support the notion that more background checks would reduce gun-related murder and suicide rates. Although Gius (2015c) and Ludwig and Cook (2000) find somewhat contrary results, it is important to note that, even in those studies, some types of background checks were associated with a decrease in either firearm homicides or suicides. Hence, universal background checks should be considered as a public policy measure to reduce gun-related murders and suicides.

Carry laws

Carry laws are laws that regulate the concealed and open carry of firearms. These laws typically refer to handguns, although long guns can also be openly carried. Concealed carry (CCW) refers to the carrying of weapons (handguns) in a concealed fashion (e.g., hidden underneath a jacket), whereas open carry (OCW) refers to the carrying of firearms openly (e.g., carrying a handgun in a holster on one's hip). Laws regulating the concealed and open carry of firearms differ substantially between states and have changed quite significantly over the past 30 years.

There are four broad types of CCW laws. The first is unrestricted; individuals in these states do not need a permit to carry a concealed handgun. For years, the only state that had no CCW restrictions was Vermont. The next type of CCW law is called a *shall-issue* law. In a shall-issue state, a permit is required to carry a concealed weapon, but state and local authorities must issue a permit to any qualified applicant who requests one. This type of CCW law is not very restrictive, and states with these laws are considered to be permissive. The third type of law is *may issue*. In a may-issue state, local and state authorities can deny requests for concealed carry permits, even requests from qualified applicants. May-issue laws restrict the ability of citizens to carry concealed weapons. Finally, there were some states that did not allow private citizens to carry concealed weapons at all; these states were known as *no-issue* or prohibited states. As of 2015, there are no prohibited states.

It is important to note that these four categories of CCW laws are rather broad, and not all states within a given category are equally restrictive. These broad categories are not definitive because the way in which a state not only interprets its statutes but also enforces them has an impact on the actual restrictiveness of the law. In addition, some cities and counties have more restrictive concealed carry laws than their home states.

As of 2015, the following nine states and the District of Columbia are may issue: (1) California, (2) Connecticut, (3) Delaware, (4) Hawaii, (5) Maryland, (6) Massachusetts, (7) New Jersey, (8) New York, and (9) Rhode Island. The following six states do not require a permit to carry a concealed handgun: (1) Alaska, (2) Arizona, (3) Kansas, (4) Maine, (5) Vermont, and (6) Wyoming. All other states require a permit but are shall issue, which is not considered restrictive.

OCW laws, in general, are more restrictive than CCW laws and have undergone less change over the past 30 years than concealed carry laws have. In addition, there are varying restrictions on OCW. For example, some states prohibit the open carry of loaded guns (California), whereas other states prohibit carrying with the intent to go armed (Tennessee) or if the purpose is to use it as a weapon against a person (Arkansas). In some states, local governments are allowed to enact more restrictive gun control measures than the state. In addition, in some states, a CCW permit allows the permit holder to carry a gun openly as well, although this is not universally true.

Unfortunately, many state statutes are silent on the open carry of firearms. Although most, if not all, states address the issue of concealed carry, many state codes make no mention of OCW. Finally, even in jurisdictions where OCW is ostensibly legal, police sometimes arrest individuals who are openly carrying firearms and charge them with disturbing the peace or a similar infraction. Hence, local and state police may discourage OCW through the use of other statutes. Therefore, given all of the aforementioned issues, determining which states actually allow OCW is rather problematic. In general, though, the overall trend over the past 30 years has been toward a slight loosening of OCW laws. It is important to note that, in 2015, some states still prohibited the open carry of handguns, whereas no states prohibited the concealed carry of handguns.

The following states and the District of Columbia prohibit the open carry of handguns: (a) California, (b) Florida, (c) Illinois, (d) New York, and (e) South Carolina. The following states require some type of permit to openly carry a handgun: (a) Connecticut, (b) Georgia, (c) Hawaii, (d) Indiana, (e) Iowa, (f) Maryland, (g) Massachusetts, (h) Minnesota, (i) Missouri, (j) New Jersey, (k) Oklahoma, (l) Rhode Island, (m) Tennessee, (n) Texas, and (o) Utah. All other states allow the open carry of handguns and do not require a permit. The laws regarding the open carry of long guns are somewhat similar.

Regarding research on the effects of CCW on crime, Table 6.1 summarizes the findings of most of the research in this area over the past 20 years. As can be seen from this table, most studies found that permissive CCW laws (shall issue or unrestricted) either reduced violent crime, or they had no significant effects on crime. Only one study (Ludwig 1998) found that permissive CCW laws increased the adult homicide rate. Some studies, such as Ayers and Donohue (2003), Donohue (2003), and Kovandzic and Marvell (2003), found that states with more permissive CCW laws had higher property crime rates. Hence, most prior research has found that permissive CCW laws either reduced violent crime or had no statistically significant effects on violent crime.

Most of the research on CCW laws was devoted to refuting or supporting the results that were found in Lott and Mustard (1997), which was one of the first studies on this topic. Using county-level data for the years 1977–1992, Lott and Mustard found that states with shall-issue CCW laws had lower crime rates than states with more restrictive gun laws. They found that shall-issue laws resulted in a 7.65% drop in murders and a 5% drop in rapes.

This result was rather controversial, and, as noted before, much of the CCW research that followed was conducted in order to find evidence either in support of or in opposition to Lott and Mustard's results. Hence, much of the research that followed Lott and Mustard used the same type of model (log-linear) and the same data (county level). In addition, most of these prior studies used panel data-estimation techniques, weighted observations, and clustered standard error corrections.

The only study that found that permissive CCW laws increased violent crime was Ludwig (1998). This study looked at the effects of shall-issue laws on violent crime rates. At the time Ludwig wrote his paper, 31 states had enacted legislation allowing for shall-issue permits. Using state-level data from 1977 to 1994, the author found that shall-issue permits increased the adult homicide rate, a finding that contradicted the results of Lott and Mustard (1997).

One of the most recent CCW studies was Gius (2014). In this study, the effects of CCW laws and assault weapons bans on gun-related murder rates were examined, and it was found that states with more restrictive CCW laws (may issue or prohibited) had higher gun-related murder rates than other states. It was also found that state-level assault weapons bans had no significant effects on gun-related murder rates.

Regarding research on OCW laws, only one study examined the effects of this type of gun control measure on violent crime (Kleck and Patterson 1993). Using city-level data for the year 1980 and a two-stage least squares model, this study found that OCW and CCW laws had no statistically significant effects on violent crimes.

Hence, research has found that the concealed and open carry of firearms (primarily handguns) either has no statistically significant effects on crime rates or that the concealed carry of firearms reduces crime. Only one study found that the concealed carry of handguns increases the crime rate.

It is important to note that we do not know how many persons legally carry firearms, either open or concealed, on a regular basis. Many studies in this area look at the restrictiveness of concealed and open carry laws without considering how many citizens actually avail themselves of this opportunity. It is reasonable to assume that states with more permissive carry laws have more citizens carrying firearms. However, there are no data on the public's knowledge of firearm carry laws nor are there any data on the percentage of persons who legally carry firearms on a regular basis. Hence, all studies, assume that a state with less restrictive carry laws have more people on the streets with guns.

Table 6.1 Summary of papers that examined effects of concealed carry laws on violent crime rates

	Permissive CCW laws reduce crime	Permissive CCW laws increase crime	Insignificant or mixed results
Ayers and Donohue 2003			X
Bartley and Cohen 1998	X		
Benson and Mast 2001	X (model specific)		
Black and Nagin 1998			X
Bronars and Lott 1998	X		
Dezhbakhsh and Rubin 1998			X
Donohue 2003			X
Duwe et al. 2002			X (examined only mass shootings)
Gius 2014	X		
Helland and Tabarrok 2004	X		
Kleck and Patterson 1993			X
Kovandzic and Marvell 2003			X (only Florida)
Kovandzic et al. 2005			X
Lott 1998	X		
Lott and Mustard 1997	X		
Ludwig 1998		X	
Moody 2001	X		
Olson and Maltz 2001	X		
Plassmann and Tideman 2001	X		
Rubin and Dezhbakhsh 2003			X

Minimum age laws and child access prevention laws

Two gun control laws that deal with children and guns are child access prevention (CAP) laws and minimum age laws. CAP laws impose criminal liabilities on adults who allow children to have unsupervised access to firearms. Although there is no federal CAP law, many states have enacted these types of laws. According to the Law Center to Prevent Gun Violence, as of 2014, 27 states and the District of Columbia have enacted some type of CAP law. Those states are as follows:

1. California	15. Mississippi
2. Colorado	16. Missouri
3. Connecticut	17. Nevada
4. Delaware	18. New Hampshire
5. Florida	19. New Jersey
6. Georgia	20. North Carolina
7. Hawaii	21. Oklahoma
8. Illinois	22. Rhode Island
9. Indiana	23. Tennessee
10. Iowa	24. Texas
11. Kentucky	25. Utah
12. Maryland	26. Virginia
13. Massachusetts	27. Wisconsin
14. Minnesota	

These laws vary widely. Some impose a criminal liability when an adult does not secure a weapon. Others only prohibit an adult from providing a firearm to a child. Many of these laws also have varying definitions of who a *minor* is. In some states, adults only have to secure firearms from children who are at most 14 years of age; for others, the age at which supervision is required is 18. Some states require secured access for all types of firearms; other states only require it for handguns. Finally, most states have exceptions for hunting, sport shooting, and other legitimate purposes.

In addition to CAP laws, many states and the federal government have laws requiring minimum ages to possess firearms, especially handguns. At the federal level, FFL dealers can only sell handguns to persons who are at least 21 years of age, and they can only sell long guns to persons who are at least 18. Nondealers (private parties) can only sell handguns to persons who are at least 18. There is no age restriction on the transfer of long guns by private parties. At the federal level, there is also a minimum age restriction of 18 on handgun possession, including handgun ammunition. There is no federal age restriction on long gun possession. Many of these federal age restrictions were part of the federal Violent Crime Control and Law Enforcement Act of 1994.

At the state level, minimum age laws are somewhat confusing. Some states have higher minimum ages than federal law for private handgun sales and handgun possession, and some states impose minimum ages for private long gun sales and long gun possession. Interestingly, though, there are some states that have lower minimum ages than that required by federal law for both handgun and long gun transfers.

Regarding research on CAP laws and minimum age laws, Marvell (2001) looked at the effects of the federal Violent Crime Control and Law Enforcement Act of 1994 on homicides and suicides. This act banned the possession of handguns by persons under 18 years of age. The authors looked at the effects of this law on both juvenile and overall homicide (1979–1998) and suicide (1976–1999) rates. Using state-level data, Marvell found that federal and state laws on the underage possession of handguns had no statistically significant effects on youth suicide rates.

Lott and Whitley (2001) examined the effects of safe-storage laws on juvenile firearm-related suicides and unintentional deaths. The authors looked at CAP laws and laws requiring some type of gun lock to be used to secure a firearm. State-level data for the period 1977–1996 were used. The authors used a fixed-effects Tobit model that included as explanatory variables a safe-storage dummy variable, non-firearm unintentional death rates, adult firearm unintentional death rates, and various control variables. Lott and Whitley found that safe storage had no significant effects on youth firearm-related unintentional deaths or suicides.

Finally, Gius (2015b) looked at the effects of CAP laws and minimum age laws on state-level suicide and unintentional death rates. Looking only at juvenile death rates, this study found that state-level minimum age laws have no significant effects on either youth suicides or unintentional deaths and that state-level CAP laws have no significant effects on unintentional deaths. States with CAP laws, however, have lower rates of youth suicide, and, after the enactment of the federal minimum age requirement, both youth suicide and unintentional death rates fell. It is uncertain why state-level minimum age laws would have no effects on juvenile suicides or unintentional deaths while federal minimum age laws resulted in a reduction in both suicides and unintentional deaths among youths.

Given the limited research and mixed results on minimum age laws and CAP laws, it is unclear if the expansion of these laws would reduce either suicides or unintentional deaths among juveniles. Two possible reasons for the lack of research in this area are (1) the paucity of data on state-level unintentional deaths and (2) the widely varying CAP statutes that exist at the state level.

Permit-to-purchase laws

The last gun control law that will be examined is the permit-to-purchase (PTP) law. These laws require prospective handgun purchasers (and in some states, long gun purchasers) to obtain a permit or license prior to the purchase of a firearm. In order to obtain a gun permit, an individual must pass a background check and, in some states, complete a firearm safety course. Most states with PTP laws also require prospective firearm owners to apply for a permit in person at a local law enforcement agency. Finally, these permits are required for sales from both licensed dealers and private sellers. Most states do not have PTP laws. As of 2011, 11 states and the District of Columbia had PTP laws. Missouri had one for several years, but it was repealed in 2007. PTP laws significantly increase the effort that is required to purchase a firearm.

States with PTP laws are as follows:

- California
- Connecticut
- District of Columbia
- Hawaii
- Illinois
- Iowa
- Massachusetts
- Michigan
- Nebraska
- New Jersey
- New York
- North Carolina

As of 2015, there have only been two studies on the impact of PTP laws on murder rates (Webster et al. 2014; Rudolph et al. 2015). In addition, one study was conducted on the effects of PTP laws on suicide rates (Crifasi et al. 2015). Regarding the homicide papers, Webster et al. (2014) examined the effects of the repeal of Missouri's PTP law on homicides. Rudolph et al. (2015) looked at Connecticut's PTP law and its effect on murder rates. The Missouri paper used a fixed-effects and correlation analysis; the Connecticut paper used the relatively new technique of a synthetic control method. Both studies found that PTP laws resulted in fewer murders. For Connecticut, it was estimated that the PTP law reduced the firearm homicide rate by 40% over a 10-year period, whereas the repeal of the Missouri PTP law resulted in a 16%–23% increase in the murder rate.

Given that so few studies have been conducted on the effects of PtP laws, it is uncertain if they reduce gun-related violent crime rates. However, both studies suggest that PTP laws are effective in reducing murder rates. Although more research is warranted in this area, there is evidence to suggest that implementation of PTP laws may reduce murder rates.

Public health research and the Dickey Amendment

The public health community has long been interested in the connection between guns and violent deaths (homicides and suicides). Although some of this research deals with the effects of gun control measures on homicides or suicides (Ludwig and Cook 2000; Conner and Zhong 2003; Fleegler et al. 2013; Irvin et al. 2014), most of the public health research on firearm violence concerns the relationship between gun ownership and homicides or suicides (Miller et al. 2002, 2006; Siegel et al. 2013, 2014a,b; Anglemyer et al. 2014; Monuteaux et al. 2015; Wintemute 2015a,b; Zeoli et al. 2016). All of this research finds that increased gun ownership levels or less restrictive gun control laws result in more firearm-related homicides and suicides. There is hardly any public health research on firearm-related violent deaths that finds that greater levels of gun ownership or less restrictive gun control laws result in fewer homicides and suicides.

The typical conclusion derived from these studies is that firearm violence is a major public health problem with 30,000 deaths annually and thousands upon thousands of others injured in firearm-related incidents. A comparison is drawn between firearm fatalities and traffic fatalities. Decades ago, traffic fatality rates were very high. Many in public health realized that something had to be done to reduce the level of traffic fatalities. More research on the issue of traffic safety was conducted. Some groups, such as the auto industry, were opposed to this research. Eventually, though, evidence-based policy proposals were implemented regarding auto safety and roadway improvements. Traffic fatalities fell precipitously.

Many in public health believe that a similar concerted effort can result in the reduction of firearm fatalities and injuries. Unfortunately, for about 20 years, there has been limited government funding for public health research in the area of firearm violence. One primary reason for this lack of government funding is the so-called Dickey Amendment, which was an amendment to the 1997 Appropriations Bill. Named after Jay Dickey, a Republican congressman from Arkansas, this amendment was in response to an article that was published in the *New England Journal of Medicine* that found that persons who owned guns were at a greater risk of being killed by a family member or a friend than persons who did not own guns. The National Rifle Association objected to the findings of the article and called for defunding the agency that supported the research (the Centers for Disease Control and Prevention's [CDC's] National Center for Injury Prevention). The agency survived, but $2.6 million was cut from their budget, which just happened to be the exact amount that the center had spent on firearm violence research in the previous year. In addition, the congressman added language stating that the CDC cannot fund any research that promotes gun control. Although not technically barring research on firearm violence, the CDC was apprehensive about their funding, and, in an abundance of caution, essentially stopped funding all firearm violence research.

It is important to note, however, that the federal government still funds some firearm violence research. For example, I recently applied for a research grant that is offered through the National Institutes of Health (NIH). The funding opportunity title for this grant was "Research on the Health Determinants and Consequences of Violence and Its Prevention, Particularly Firearm Violence." Although the total amount to be awarded is unknown (it is contingent upon NIH appropriations), it is a mischaracterization to state that the federal government does not fund any research in the area of firearm violence. In addition, many nongovernment organizations, such as The Joyce Foundation, support research in the area of firearm violence. Finally, many academics who receive no outside funding whatsoever, such as myself, conduct research in this area. Hence, the extent of the impact of the Dickey Amendment on gun control and firearm violence research is uncertain.

Politics and gun control

Gun control is a very sensitive topic in American politics. For the past half-century, Democrats have been for gun control, and Republicans have been against it. States that have large Democratic majorities typically have much stricter gun control laws than states with large Republican majorities. There are some glaring exceptions (Texas did not allow the open carry of handguns until very recently), but, in general, these generalizations have remained true for a very long time.

It was not always the case, though, that Republicans did not favor gun control. For example, in 1967, Assemblyman Don Mulford, a Republican from Alameda County, put forth a bill in the California State Assembly that would, among other things, prohibit the carrying of loaded firearms in public. At the time, the Black Panthers, a militant African-American organization, was active in California, and its members typically carried guns in public. Upon learning of this impending legislation, the Black Panthers decided to protest the Mulford Bill. So, on May 2, 1967, several cars pulled up to the state Capitol in Sacramento, and about 30 young African-Americans armed with rifles and shotguns emerged from their vehicles and started walking toward the Capitol building. The protesters entered the Capitol with their loaded guns plainly visible. In California in the late 1960s, it was not illegal to carry a loaded gun in public, and there was no law banning loaded guns in the Capitol building the police allowed the Black Panthers to enter the Capitol building. About 12 of the protestors then proceeded to the Assembly Chamber where the lawmakers were in session. They were able to gain access to the chamber but were quickly escorted out, primarily because the rules of the Assembly forbade weapons in the Assembly. The police finally stopped the Black Panthers as they were exiting the building. At first, the police confiscated some of the firearms but then returned them because no law was being violated. After the Black Panthers drove off and were a few blocks away from the Capitol building, they were stopped again by police. This time, some of the protesters were arrested for carrying loaded guns in a car, and others were held for questioning.

While this somewhat bizarre incident was transpiring, the newly elected Governor, Ronald Reagan, was just about to enjoy a picnic lunch at the Capitol with a group of eighth-grade students. They were on their way out of the building when the Black Panthers were just leaving the state Capitol. It must have been an interesting scene with the governor and a group of middle-school students milling about the grounds of the Capitol along with about 30 armed Black Panthers. Reagan was even heard to exclaim that "There's no reason why on the street today the citizen should be carrying loaded weapons" (*The Sacramento Bee* 1967, p. A10). The Mulford Bill passed, and Governor Reagan signed it into law. It is still illegal in California to carry a loaded gun in public.

This incident illustrates the fact that, sometimes, gun control support crosses party lines. Of course, there have also been incidents when Democratic governors and legislators were not in support of more restrictive gun control measures. Unfortunately, given the polarization of politics in America at present, there is very little cross-party support for either more restrictive or less restrictive gun control measures. This is unfortunate because, as noted earlier in this chapter, there are some gun control measures that research has shown may reduce gun-related murders and other violent crimes. Granted, the data used in many of these studies are less than ideal. Nonetheless, when the majority of research illustrates that certain policies may reduce crime, every effort should be made to verify these results and to structure laws to protect Second Amendment rights and reduce gun violence.

chapter seven

International comparisons of homicides and guns

A common argument among gun control advocates is that homicide rates, and especially gun-related homicide rates, are much higher in the United States than they are in the rest of the world. They contend that this is true because of the easy availability of firearms and the lax gun control laws that exist in the United States. Gun control opponents, however, contend that our homicide rates are not that much higher than the rest of the world and that there is little correlation between firearm availability and homicide rates. In order to assess the validity of these claims, international data on firearms and homicide are presented on Tables 7.1 through 7.5. All of the crime data were obtained from the United Nations Office of Drugs and Crime. All of the firearm data were obtained from the *Small Arms Survey*.

Although not all countries are represented in the tables, there are several interesting observations that can be made. First, the United States does not have a very high homicide rate compared to the rest of the world. In 2012, the United States had a homicide rate of 4.7 homicides per 100,000 persons. This is 69th out of 156 countries. Countries that had much higher homicide rates include Costa Rica (8.5), Peru (9.6), Ecuador (12.4), Grenada (13.3), Panama (17.2), Mexico (21.5), Puerto Rico (26.5), Bahamas (29.8), and Belize (44.7). Many of these countries are popular tourist destinations, and some have rather large expat retiree communities. Granted, there were 68 countries that had lower homicide rates. Most of Europe did, but Libya (1.7), Liberia (3.2), and Iran (4.1) also had lower homicide rates.

Regarding the prevalence of gun-related homicides, the United States ranked 41st out of 59 countries in 2011. Hence, 48 countries had lower percentages of homicides that were gun related. In the United States, 59% of homicides were gun related. In most European countries, the percentage of homicides due to guns was much lower. Examples include United Kingdom (7%), Austria (10%), Czech Republic (11%), Spain (14%), Denmark (34%), and Switzerland (48%). Countries that had higher percentages include Slovenia (63%), Belize (67%), Bahamas (74%), and Panama (76%).

Data on civilian gun ownership are rather difficult to obtain. Very few countries maintain national registries of firearms. Most data on gun ownership are estimates based on surveys. One of the best sources of data on

Table 7.1 Homicide rates by country, homicides per 100,000 persons

Country	2007	2008	2009	2010	2011	2012
Afghanistan			4	3.5	4.2	6.5
Albania	3.3	2.9	2.7	4	4.5	5
Algeria	0.8	0.9	0.8	0.7	0.7	
Andorra	0	1.3	1.3	1.3		
Angola						10
Anguilla	30.4	7.5				
Antigua and Barbuda	20.1	18.7	18.5	6.9		11.2
Argentina	5.3	5.8	5.5	5.5		
Armenia	2.6	2.8	2.8	1.5	2.2	1.8
Aruba	5.9	4.9	3.9	3.9		
Australia	1.2	1.2	1.2	1	1.1	1.1
Austria	0.5	0.5	0.5	0.6	0.8	0.9
Azerbaijan	2	1.9	1.8	2.1		
Bahamas	22.8	21	24.5	26.1	34.7	29.8
Bahrain	0.4	0.5	1.1	0.9	0.5	
Bangladesh	2.6	2.8	2.8	2.6		2.7
Barbados	9.8	9	6.8	11.1	9.6	7.4
Belarus	6.8	5.7	5	5.1		
Belgium	2	1.9	1.7	1.7	1.9	1.6
Belize	33.9	35.1	32.2	41.8	39.2	44.7
Benin						8.4
Bermuda	4.7	7.7	9.3	10.8	12.3	7.7
Bhutan	1.2	1	1.1	1.7		
Bolivia	8.1	8.6	8.4	10.4	10	12.1
Bosnia and Herzegovina			1.8	1.5	1.3	
Botswana						18.4
Brazil	23.5	23.9	23	22.2	23.4	25.2
British Virgin Islands						
Brunei Darussalam						2
Bulgaria	2.3	2.3	2	2	1.7	1.9
Burkina Faso						8
Burundi						8
Cabo Verde		6.4	6.2	10.7	15.1	10.3
Cambodia						6.5
Cameroon						7.6
Canada	1.6	1.7	1.6	1.4	1.5	1.6
Cayman Islands	3.9	7.6	14.7			

(*Continued*)

Table 7.1 (Continued) Homicide rates by country, homicides per 100,000 persons

Country	2007	2008	2009	2010	2011	2012
Central African Republic						11.8
Chad						7.3
Chile	3.7	3.5	3.7	3.2	3.7	3.1
China	1.2	1.1	1.1	1		
Colombia	34.7	33	33.7	32.3	33.6	30.8
Comoros						10
Congo						12.5
Cook Islands						3.1
Costa Rica	8.3	11.3	11.4	11.3	10	8.5
Côte d'Ivoire						13.6
Croatia	1.4	1.5	1.1	1.4	1.1	1.2
Cuba						4.2
Cyprus	1.2	0.8	1.7	0.7	0.8	2
Czech Republic	1.2	1.1	0.9	1	0.8	1
Democratic People's Republic of Korea						5.2
Democratic Republic of the Congo						28.3
Denmark	0.7	1	0.9	0.8	0.8	0.8
Djibouti						10.1
Dominica	9.9	9.9	18.3	21.1		
Dominican Republic	22	24.6	24	24.7	24.8	22.1
Ecuador	15.9	18	17.8	17.6	15.4	12.4
Egypt	0.9	1.3	1.2	2.4	3.4	
El Salvador	57.1	51.7	70.9	64.1	69.9	41.2
Equatorial Guinea						19.3
Eritrea						7.1
Estonia	7.1	6.4	5.4	5.4	5	
Ethiopia						12
Fiji						4
Finland	2.5	2.5	2.2	2.2	2.1	1.6
France	1.3	1.3	1.1	1.1	1.2	1
French Guiana	13.1	14.5	13.3			
French Polynesia	2.7	3.4	0.4			
Gabon						9.1
Gambia						10.2
Georgia	7.5	6	4.8	4.3		

(Continued)

Table 7.1 (Continued) Homicide rates by country, homicides per 100,000 persons

Country	2007	2008	2009	2010	2011	2012
Germany	0.9	0.9	0.8	0.8	0.8	
Ghana						6.1
Greece	1.2	1.3	1.3	1.6	1.7	
Greenland	3.5	10.6	19.4			
Grenada	10.6	15.4	6.7	9.6	3.8	13.3
Guadeloupe	6.4	7.1	7.9			
Guam	0.6	0.6	3.2	1.9	2.5	
Guatemala	43.4	46.1	46.5	41.6	38.6	39.9
Guinea						8.9
Guinea-Bissau						8.4
Guyana	14.9	20.4	15	17.8	16.4	17
Haiti	5.1	5.2	6.1	6.8	9.1	10.2
Honduras	50	60.8	70.7	81.8	91.4	90.4
Hong Kong	0.3	0.5	0.7	0.5	0.2	0.4
Hungary	1.5	1.5	1.4	1.3	1.4	1.3
Iceland	0.7	0	0.3	0.6	0.9	0.3
India	3.6	3.6	3.5	3.5	3.6	3.5
Indonesia		0.6	0.6	0.4	0.6	0.6
Iran						4.1
Iraq						8
Ireland	1.8	1.1	1.3	1.2	0.9	1.2
Israel	1.8	1.9	1.8	2	2	1.8
Italy	1.1	1	1	0.9	0.9	0.9
Jamaica	58.5	59.5	61.6	52.6	41.1	39.3
Japan	0.5	0.5	0.4	0.4	0.3	
Jordan	1.7	1.7	1.5	1.7	2	
Kazakhstan	10.8	10.5	10.2	8.7	8.8	7.8
Kenya	3.4	3.6	5.6	5.5	6.3	6.4
Kiribati						8.2
Kosovo		4.4	3.2	3.6		
Kuwait						0.4
Kyrgyzstan	8.3	8.3	8	20.1	9.1	
Lao People's Democratic Republic						5.9
Latvia	4.3	4.6	5.1	3.3	3.3	4.7
Lebanon	2.6	6	1.9	2.2		

(Continued)

Table 7.1 (Continued) Homicide rates by country, homicides
per 100,000 persons

Country	2007	2008	2009	2010	2011	2012
Lesotho	45.8	38.1	36.3	38		
Liberia	2.8	4.8	3.8	3.3	3.9	3.2
Libya						1.7
Liechtenstein	0	2.8	0	2.8	0	0
Lithuania	8.7	9.5	8.1	7.1	6.9	6.7
Luxembourg	1.5	1.6	1	2	0.8	
Macedonia	2	1.7	1.7	2	1.4	
Madagascar						11.1
Malawi	5	5.5	2.2	3.5	2.2	1.8
Malaysia						2.3
Maldives						3.9
Mali						7.5
Malta	1	1.4	0.9	0.9	0.7	2.8
Marshall Islands						4.7
Martinique	5.8	4.3	2.7			
Mauritania						5
Mauritius			3.1	2.7	2.8	
Mayotte	14.5	2.6	6			
Mexico	7.8	12.2	17	21.8	22.8	21.5
Micronesia (Federated States of)						4.6
Monaco	0	0				
Mongolia	11.3	8.1	8.2	8.8	9.7	
Montenegro	1.9	3.9	3.4	2.4	3.4	2.7
Montserrat		20.4				
Morocco	1.7	1.4	1.4	1.4	1.4	2.2
Mozambique						12.4
Myanmar						15.2
Namibia		16.8	18.1	14.4	13.9	17.2
Nauru						1.3
Nepal	3.4	3.4	3	3	2.9	
Netherlands	0.9	0.9	0.9	0.9	0.9	0.9
New Caledonia	5.1	4.6	3.3			
New Zealand	1.1	1.2	1.5	1	0.9	0.9
Nicaragua	12.8	13	14	13.5	12.5	11.3
Niger						4.7

(Continued)

Table 7.1 (Continued) Homicide rates by country, homicides per 100,000 persons

Country	2007	2008	2009	2010	2011	2012
Nigeria						20
Niue						3.6
Norway	0.6	0.7	0.6	0.6	2.2	
Oman	0.7	0.7			1.1	
Pakistan	6.4	7.2	7.3	7.6	7.9	7.7
Palau						3.1
Panama	12.7	18.4	22.6	20.6	20.3	17.2
Papua New Guinea	8.1	9.2	10.4	10.4		
Paraguay	12.8	13.4	12.9	11.5	10	9.7
Peru	10.4	11.6	10.3	9.3	9.6	9.6
Philippines	6.5	6.4	6.9	9.5	9.1	8.8
Poland	1.4	1.2	1.3	1.1	1.2	
Portugal	1.8	1.2	1.2	1.2	1.1	1.2
Puerto Rico	19.6	21.6	24	26.5		26.5
Qatar						1.1
Republic of Korea					0.9	
Republic of Moldova	5.9	6.5	6.8	7.5	8.6	6.5
Réunion	3	2.2	1.8			
Romania	1.9	2.1	1.8	1.8	1.5	1.7
Russian Federation		11.6	11.1	10.1	9.6	9.2
Rwanda						23.1
Saint Kitts and Nevis	31.7	45	52.2	40.1	64.2	33.6
Saint Lucia	17	22.6	22.3	24.8		21.6
Saint Pierre and Miquelon	0	16.5	16.5			
Saint Vincent and the Grenadines	33	14.7	18.3	22.9	19.2	25.6
Samoa						3.6
San Marino						0.7
Sao Tome and Principe	2.4	8.3	2.9	3.4	3.3	
Saudi Arabia						0.8
Senegal						2.8
Serbia	1.7	1.4	1.5	1.3	1.4	1.2
Seychelles						9.5
Sierra Leone	2.5	3.3	2.8	2.8	3.2	1.9
Singapore	0.4	0.6	0.4	0.4	0.3	0.2
Slovakia	1.6	1.7	1.5	1.6	1.8	1.4

(Continued)

Table 7.1 (Continued) Homicide rates by country, homicides
per 100,000 persons

Country	2007	2008	2009	2010	2011	2012
Slovenia	1.2	0.5	0.6	0.7	0.8	0.7
Solomon Islands						4.3
Somalia						8
South Africa	37.3	36.1	33.1	31	30	31
South Sudan						13.9
Spain	1.1	0.9	0.9	0.8	0.8	0.8
Sri Lanka	8.2	7.3	4.7	3.6	3.4	
State of Palestine						7.4
Sudan						11.2
Suriname						6.1
Swaziland						33.8
Sweden	1.2	0.8	0.9	1	0.9	0.7
Switzerland	0.7	0.7	0.7	0.7	0.6	
Syria	2.8	2.7	2.4	2.2		
Taiwan	3.8	3.5	3.6	3.2	3	
Tajikistan	1.9	1.4	1.3	2.4	1.6	
Tanzania						12.7
Thailand	6.7	6	5.6	5.5	5	
Timor-Leste	6	3.3	3	3.6		
Togo						10.3
Tonga	1	3.9	7.7	1	1.9	1
Trinidad and Tobago	29.8	41.6	38.3	35.6	26.4	28.3
Tunisia						2.2
Turkey	3.7	3.3	3.3	2.7	2.6	
Turkmenistan						12.8
Turks and Caicos Islands		6.8	6.6			
Tuvalu						4.2
Uganda	8.6	8.8	9.8	9.3	10.7	
Ukraine	5.7	5.2	4.7	4.3		
United Arab Emirates				0.8	0.6	0.7
United Kingdom	1.4	1.2	1.2	1.2	1	
United States of America	5.6	5.4	5	4.7	4.7	4.7
Uruguay	5.8	6.6	6.7	6.1	5.9	7.9
Uzbekistan						3.7
Vanuatu						2.9
Venezuela	47.6	51.9	48.9	45	47.8	53.7

(Continued)

Table 7.1 (Continued) Homicide rates by country, homicides
per 100,000 persons

Country	2007	2008	2009	2010	2011	2012
Vietnam						3.3
Yemen	4	4	4.5	4.8		
Zambia						10.7
Zimbabwe						10.6

Source: Courtesy of Office of Drugs and Crime, United Nations.
Note: Blanks indicate no data available for that country and year.

Table 7.2 Percentage of homicides committed with gun

Country	2007	2008	2009	2010	2011	2012
Albania	63%	60%	67%	69%	61%	
Algeria	5%	6%				
Andorra	0%	100%	0%	0%		
Argentina	46%	48%				
Armenia	29%	22%	11%	23%	9%	11%
Australia	13%	12%	13%	17%	17%	17%
Austria	11%	7%	9%	9%	10%	
Azerbaijan	13%	7%		13%		
Bahamas	55%	63%	60%	73%	74%	
Bahrain	25%	0%				
Belarus	3%	3%	3%			
Belize			49%	62%	67%	
Bolivia				7%		
Bosnia and Herzegovina	55%	12%	49%	46%	14%	
Brunei Darussalam						
Bulgaria	31%	30%	29%	22%	32%	18%
Canada	35%	36%	32%	34%	29%	
Chile	7%	9%	25%	23%	27%	
Colombia	71%	71%	78%	78%	77%	
Costa Rica	61%	68%	64%	66%	63%	64%
Croatia	47%	38%	35%	45%	27%	31%
Cyprus	23%	33%	26%	13%	33%	52%
Czech Republic	14%	15%	15%	6%	11%	10%

(Continued)

Table 7.2 (Continued) Percentage of homicides committed with gun

Country	2007	2008	2009	2010	2011	2012
Denmark	18%	11%	26%	26%	34%	
Dominican Republic		70%	65%	65%	63%	64%
Ecuador						
Egypt	43%	49%	43%	23%	68%	
El Salvador	80%	67%	76%	73%	70%	62%
England and Wales	7%	6%	7%	10%	7%	
Finland	19%	23%	20%	12%	14%	19%
Georgia	14%	17%	16%	13%		
Germany						
Grenada	18%	6%	0%	0%	0%	0%
Guatemala	83%	83%	83%			
Guyana			10%	21%	25%	
Honduras		79%	81%	83%	84%	
Hong Kong	0%	0%	0%	0%		
Hungary	8%	8%	5%	11%	9%	7%
Iceland	50%	0%	0%	0%	0%	0%
India	12%	10%	7%	7%		
Italy			41%			
Jamaica	79%	77%	77%	76%	70%	
Jordan						
Kazakhstan	5%	5%	7%	7%	7%	7%
Korea					2%	
Kyrgyzstan	2%	3%	4%	3%	1%	
Latvia	4%	8%	5%	6%		
Lebanon						
Liechtenstein	0%	100%	0%	0%	0%	
Lithuania	3%	1%	3%	1%	1%	
Luxembourg	29%	13%	40%	0%	0%	
Macedonia	62%	49%	37%	65%	63%	
Maldives	67%	100%				
Malta	50%	83%	0%	50%	0%	42%
Mauritius	0%	0%	0%	3%	0%	
Mexico	39%	39%	55%	55%	57%	
Moldova	3%	3%	3%	2%	4%	5%
Monaco						
Mongolia	6%	6%	5%	2%	2%	
Montenegro	67%	33%	52%	47%	76%	

(Continued)

Table 7.2 (Continued) Percentage of homicides committed with gun

Country	2007	2008	2009	2010	2011	2012
Namibia		19%	18%	14%	13%	15%
Nepal						
Netherlands	28%	25%	27%	23%	34%	
New Zealand	13%	14%	16%	16%	8%	7%
Nicaragua				52%		
Northern Ireland	14%	4%	17%	13%	22%	
Panama	65%	79%	82%	77%	76%	74%
Paraguay	61%	62%	57%	62%	61%	64%
Peru	20%	16%	18%			
Poland	10%	7%	7%	7%	5%	
Portugal	29%	44%	34%	36%	20%	37%
Romania	2%	1%	1%	1%	3%	2%
Saint Kitts and Nevis			85%	81%	88%	
Saint Vincent and the Grenadines	58%		30%	36%		
Sao Tome and Principe	100%	100%	100%	100%	100%	
Serbia	25%	35%	31%	28%	20%	12%
Sierra Leone		70%				
Singapore	0%	0%	0%	0%	0%	
Slovakia	20%	19%	17%	19%	14%	19%
Slovenia	38%	20%	15%	40%	63%	29%
Solomon Islands	0%	0%				
South Africa	33%					
South Sudan						14%
Spain	14%	16%	23%	18%	14%	14%
State of Palestine						
Sweden				17%		
Switzerland			47%	25%	48%	
Tajikistan	14%	9%	16%	10%	10%	
Tonga	0%	25%	0%	0%	0%	0%
Trinidad and Tobago	78%	79%	72%	75%	71%	
Turkey						
Uganda	9%	13%	11%	19%		
Ukraine	3%	3%	5%			
United States of America	59%	58%	60%	60%	59%	60%
Uruguay					49%	

Source: Courtesy of Office of Drugs and Crime, United Nations.

Note: Blanks indicate no data available for that country and year.

Table 7.3 Comparison of homicide rates and percentage gun related, 2011

Country	Homicide rate (homicides per 100,000 persons)	Percentage of homicides gun related
Albania	4.5	61%
Armenia	2.2	9%
Australia	1.1	17%
Austria	0.8	10%
Bahamas	31.7	74%
Belize	39.2	67%
Bosnia and Herzegovina	1.3	14%
Bulgaria	1.7	32%
Canada	1.5	29%
Chile	3.7	27%
Colombia	33.6	77%
Costa Rica	10	63%
Croatia	1.1	27%
Cyprus	0.8	33%
Czech Republic	0.8	11%
Denmark	0.8	34%
Dominican Republic	24.8	63%
Egypt	3.4	68%
El Salvador	69.9	70%
Finland	2.1	14%
Grenada	3.8	0%
Guyana	16.4	25%
Honduras	91.4	84%
Hungary	1.4	9%
Iceland	0.9	0%
Jamaica	41.1	70%
Kazakhstan	8.8	7%
Kyrgyzstan	9.1	1%
Liechtenstein	0	0%
Lithuania	6.9	1%
Luxembourg	0.8	0%
Macedonia	1.4	63%
Malta	0.7	0%
Mauritius	2.8	0%
Mexico	22.8	57%
Mongolia	9.7	2%

(Continued)

Table 7.3 (Continued) Comparison of homicide rates and percentage gun
related, 2011

Country	Homicide rate (homicides per 100,000 persons)	Percentage of homicides gun related
Montenegro	3.4	76%
Namibia	13.9	13%
Netherlands	0.9	34%
New Zealand	0.9	8%
Panama	20.3	76%
Paraguay	10	61%
Poland	1.2	5%
Portugal	1.1	20%
Romania	1.5	3%
Saint Kitts and Nevis	64.2	88%
Sao Tome and Principe	3.3	100%
Serbia	1.4	20%
Singapore	0.3	0%
Slovakia	1.8	14%
Slovenia	0.8	63%
Spain	0.8	14%
Switzerland	0.6	48%
Tajikistan	1.6	10%
Tonga	1.9	0%
Trinidad and Tobago	26.4	71%
United Kingdom	1	7%
United States of America	4.7	59%
Uruguay	5.9	49%

Source: Courtesy of Office of Drugs and Crime, United Nations.

civilian firearm ownership is the *Small Arms Survey*, which is an annual
publication that presents data and research on various aspects of firearms.
The latest issue that presents data on civilian gun ownership in various
countries is the 2007 edition. Table 7.6 is a table that was partially repro-
duced from that report.

Although these are only estimates, the data show that the United
States is the most heavily armed nation in the world. In fact, there are
almost as many guns as people in the United States. Most nations in
Europe have rates of gun ownership that are less than half what they are
in the United States. England's gun ownership rate is less than one-tenth
of the U.S. rate. There appears to be little relationship between guns and

Table 7.4 Percentage of homicide victims that are male

Country	2007	2008	2009	2010	2011	2012
Albania	77.10%	79.60%	91.80%	85.00%	87.30%	83.40%
Andorra	0.00%	0.00%	0.00%	100.00%		0.00%
Armenia	83.10%	69.90%	69.90%	77.30%	74.60%	64.80%
Australia	65.70%	61.50%	71.80%	61.30%	64.80%	67.30%
Austria	61.70%	66.70%	63.80%	60.60%	60.70%	59.80%
Azerbaijan				69.90%		
Bahamas	89.70%	90.40%	88.50%	85.10%	87.40%	
Barbados			78.90%	67.70%		
Belarus	65.90%	66.80%	59.30%			
Belize			90.70%	87.50%	90.30%	
Bosnia and Herzegovina			78.90%	69.60%	68.60%	
Bulgaria	78.50%	79.10%	76.70%	81.60%	76.60%	82.30%
Canada	72.00%	74.80%	72.00%	71.40%	69.80%	
Chile	82.00%	82.50%	84.20%	82.30%	81.90%	
Colombia	91.90%	92.20%	92.00%	92.00%	91.60%	
Costa Rica	90.00%	88.30%	88.80%	88.40%	86.50%	87.70%
Croatia	61.30%	66.20%	51.00%	48.40%	57.10%	64.70%
Cyprus	76.90%	77.80%	63.20%	87.50%	33.30%	77.30%
Czech Republic	56.30%	61.40%	59.60%	48.50%	48.80%	54.30%
Denmark				47.60%	67.40%	66.00%
Dominican Republic				91.00%	90.50%	91.10%
Egypt	76.00%	79.40%	78.80%	89.30%	87.80%	
El Salvador	90.30%	90.00%	86.50%	85.90%	85.60%	89.00%
Estonia	80.00%	78.00%	69.50%	76.60%		
Fiji	14.30%	41.20%				
Finland	62.30%	66.90%	71.70%	77.60%	66.70%	53.90%
Georgia	86.40%	83.70%	84.20%	85.00%	75.70%	
Germany	52.20%	53.30%	50.40%	48.00%	52.70%	
Greece	90.70%	97.00%	93.40%			
Grenada	81.80%	87.50%	57.10%	80.00%	75.00%	64.30%
Guatemala	89.80%	89.10%	88.90%			
Guyana	75.70%	75.90%	75.20%	77.90%	60.00%	
Honduras			93.10%		93.20%	
Hong Kong	38.90%	30.60%	46.80%	45.70%	47.10%	
Hungary	59.10%	60.30%	54.70%	57.90%	71.80%	58.30%

(Continued)

Table 7.4 (Continued) Percentage of homicide victims that are male

Country	2007	2008	2009	2010	2011	2012
Iceland	100.00%	0.00%	100.00%	100.00%	66.70%	0.00%
India	61.00%	61.00%	58.80%	59.50%	58.90%	59.20%
Ireland	81.20%	81.80%	86.70%	86.70%	86.70%	86.70%
Italy	76.30%	76.00%	70.70%	70.80%	69.90%	
Jamaica	90.50%	89.80%	90.70%	90.00%	89.50%	
Japan	50.90%	47.80%	50.00%	49.00%	47.10%	
Kyrgyzstan	76.40%	79.10%	68.70%			
Latvia						49.00%
Liechtenstein				100.00%		
Lithuania	74.00%	72.80%	74.60%	65.80%	68.70%	73.80%
Luxembourg	57.10%	50.00%	100.00%	50.00%	100.00%	
Macedonia	73.80%	74.30%	65.70%	65.10%	86.70%	
Malawi	13.00%	65.50%	34.70%	69.20%	48.10%	87.50%
Malta	75.00%	83.30%	25.00%	75.00%	0.00%	75.00%
Mauritius			57.90%	75.80%	76.50%	
Moldova	68.70%	61.40%	71.10%	79.80%	81.60%	72.50%
Mongolia	77.50%	76.90%	73.10%	72.00%	77.40%	
Montenegro	75.00%	79.20%	68.20%	53.30%	85.70%	82.40%
Morocco			87.80%			
New Zealand	60.40%	54.90%	62.70%	47.60%	61.50%	48.80%
Nicaragua				90.10%		
Norway	43.30%	70.60%	58.60%	48.30%	53.20%	
Panama	92.50%	93.70%	91.30%	92.50%	95.30%	94.60%
Philippines	84.00%	79.40%	82.70%	86.00%	88.00%	
Romania	63.20%	60.60%	63.00%	62.50%		
Saint Kitts and Nevis			88.90%	90.50%		
Saint Vincent and the Grenadines	77.80%	81.30%	85.00%	88.00%		
Serbia	67.80%	72.90%	76.60%	66.70%	72.00%	64.90%
Singapore	72.20%	59.30%	65.00%	84.20%	62.50%	
Slovakia	65.90%	72.10%	59.00%			
Slovenia	66.70%	50.00%	46.20%	46.70%	56.30%	57.10%
South Africa	85.40%	85.90%	84.50%	82.70%	84.60%	
South Korea					47.50%	
South Sudan						82.50%
Spain			66.90%	61.00%	66.80%	65.70%

(Continued)

Table 7.4 (Continued) Percentage of homicide victims that are male

Country	2007	2008	2009	2010	2011	2012
Sweden				68.10%		
Switzerland			47.10%	50.00%	50.00%	
Tajikistan	75.00%	62.00%	75.00%	87.30%	86.50%	
Tonga	100.00%	75.00%	62.50%	100.00%	100.00%	0.00%
Trinidad and Tobago	92.30%	90.30%	92.50%	88.70%	91.70%	
Turkey	80.50%	81.10%	79.00%	77.70%	79.50%	
Uganda		86.20%				
Ukraine	73.20%	74.90%	72.40%	68.60%		
United Kingdom	73.80%	69.70%	69.00%	69.60%	70.30%	
United States of America	78.50%	78.20%	77.10%	77.50%	77.80%	77.80%
Zambia				77.80%		

Source: Office of Drugs and Crime, United Nations.

Note: Blanks indicate no data available for that country and year.

crime. In 2007, the United States had a homicide rate of 5.6 and a gun ownership rate of 88.8. However, Switzerland had a homicide rate of 0.7 and a gun ownership rate of 45.7. Finland had a homicide rate of 2.5 and a gun ownership rate of 45.3. But Belize had a homicide rate of 33.9 and a gun ownership rate of 10. Brazil had a homicide rate of 23.5 and a gun ownership rate of 8. Hence, lower gun ownership rates do not necessarily translate into lower homicide rates, and higher gun ownership rates do not translate into higher murder rates.

There are several problems with international comparisons of homicide rates and gun ownership rates. First, many gun ownership rates are estimates. There are very few countries that maintain accurate and complete records of civilian gun ownership. Second, for many less developed countries, homicide data are not reliable. Finally, there are many other factors that affect crime besides gun ownership. By merely comparing gun ownership rates and homicide rates, one is not taking into account the myriad cultural, economic, and social factors that may affect homicide rates in any given country. For example, even if it were possible to eliminate all firearm-related homicides in the United States, the homicide rate in 2014 would still be approximately 1.28 homicides per 100,000 persons, which is very comparable to the homicide rate in many European countries. This estimate does not take account the possibility that some murderers would use different weapons. Hence, the homicide rate in a

Table 7.5 Percentage of homicides that are gang related

Country	2007	2008	2009	2010	2011	2012
Armenia	3.90%	1.20%	4.80%	0.00%	0.00%	0.00%
Australia	3.90%	2.30%	1.90%			
Azerbaijan				1.50%		
Bahamas	42.30%	43.80%	49.40%	68.10%	65.40%	
Barbados	24.00%	4.30%	15.80%	9.70%		
Belize	13.40%	14.60%	11.30%	37.20%		
Bulgaria	2.80%	1.20%	3.30%	2.70%	1.60%	1.40%
Canada	42.30%	48.60%	45.20%	37.00%	34.40%	
Colombia	4.30%	3.80%	8.20%	9.10%	5.60%	
Costa Rica		33.20%	31.40%	35.10%	37.10%	
Dominican Republic				2.40%	2.50%	0.80%
El Salvador	3.60%	1.40%	8.90%	15.70%	5.90%	16.80%
Finland	0.00%	0.80%	0.00%	0.90%	1.80%	
France	7.00%	15.00%				
Grenada	0.00%	6.30%	28.60%	20.00%	0.00%	0.00%
Honduras	21.10%	36.90%	33.80%	34.80%		
Hong Kong	1.10%	0.60%				
Hungary	0.60%	0.00%	1.40%	0.00%	0.00%	0.80%
Italy	18.90%	17.20%	15.30%	13.00%	9.60%	
Jamaica	50.50%	45.40%	52.40%	27.60%	50.00%	
Japan	20.40%	22.60%				
Luxembourg	14.30%	12.50%	40.00%	0.00%	0.00%	
Macedonia		2.90%				
Mexico	27.60%	51.80%				
Mongolia	5.50%	5.70%	4.60%	1.70%	0.00%	
Netherlands	7.00%	12.00%	11.00%			
Nicaragua		4.20%	4.40%			
Panama	31.30%	53.20%	45.70%	24.90%	37.00%	52.10%
Poland			3.20%	2.50%	2.20%	
Saint Kitts and Nevis	37.50%	39.10%	70.40%			
Spain					1.00%	1.60%
Sri Lanka						
Sweden				13.20%		
Timor-Leste				5.10%		
Trinidad and Tobago	52.70%	49.40%	30.60%	15.90%	26.40%	

(Continued)

Table 7.5 (Continued) Percentage of homicides that are gang related

Country	2007	2008	2009	2010	2011	2012
United States of America	4.40%	5.10%	5.80%	5.80%	4.60%	
Uruguay					13.10%	
Zambia	1.50%	6.80%	2.80%	4.60%		

Source: Courtesy of Office of Drugs and Crime, United Nations.
Note: Blanks indicate no data available for that country and year.

Table 7.6 Civilian gun ownership, 2007

Country	Firearms per 100 persons
United States of America	88.8
Yemen	54.8
Switzerland	45.7
Finland	45.3
Serbia	37.8
Cyprus	36.4
Saudi Arabia	35.0
Iraq	34.2
Uruguay	31.8
Sweden	31.6
Norway	31.3
France	31.2
Canada	30.8
Austria	30.4
Iceland	30.3
Germany	30.3
Oman	25.4
Bahrain	24.8
Kuwait	24.8
Macedonia	24.1
Montenegro	23.1
New Zealand	22.6
Greece	22.5
United Arab Emirates	22.1
Northern Ireland	21.9
Croatia	21.7
Panama	21.7

(Continued)

Table 7.6 (Continued) Civilian gun ownership, 2007

Country	Firearms per 100 persons
Lebanon	21.0
Equatorial Guinea	19.9
Kosovo	19.5
Qatar	19.2
Latvia	19.0
Peru	18.8
Angola	17.3
Bosnia-Herzegovina	17.3
Belgium	17.2
Paraguay	17.0
Czech Republic	16.3
Thailand	15.6
Libya	15.5
Gabon	14.0
Slovenia	13.5
Suriname	13.4
Guatemala	13.1
South Africa	12.7
Namibia	12.6
Armenia	12.5
Turkey	12.5
Denmark	12.0
Italy	11.9
Malta	11.9
Pakistan	11.6
Jordan	11.5
Chile	10.7
Venezuela	10.7
Spain	10.4
Argentina	10.2
Belize	10.0
Costa Rica	9.9
Estonia	9.2
Somalia	9.1
Russia	8.9
Zambia	8.9
Albania	8.6

(*Continued*)

Table 7.6 (Continued) Civilian gun ownership, 2007

Country	Firearms per 100 persons
Ireland	8.6
Portugal	8.5
Slovakia	8.3
Jamaica	8.1
Brazil	8.0
Barbados	7.8
Nicaragua	7.7
Algeria	7.6
Belarus	7.3
Georgia	7.3
Iran	7.3
Israel	7.3
Moldova	7.1
Ukraine	6.6
Maldives	6.5
Kenya	6.4
Swaziland	6.4
Bulgaria	6.2
England and Wales	6.2
Honduras	6.2
Colombia	5.9
El Salvador	5.8
Hungary	5.5
Scotland	5.5
Sudan	5.5
Cape Verde	5.4

Source: Small Arms Survey, 2007.

gun-free America would probably still be higher than the homicide rate in many European countries. Given the complexity surrounding criminal behavior, and murder in particular, international comparisons of gun ownership and homicide rates are not very informative and may actually prevent researchers from focusing on the true causes of crime.

chapter eight

Evidence-based solutions and a proposal to reduce firearm violence

I finally obtained my Connecticut Pistol Permit. I received a letter on February 25 notifying me that my application for a Connecticut State Pistol Permit had been approved and that I could pick up my temporary permit at the local police department. The temporary permit was valid for only 60 days. During that period, I had to go to the State Police Headquarters in order to obtain my permanent permit. I went on March 3. There was a short line. I had to fill out yet another form, an application for a pistol permit. One of the more interesting questions on the form was *Reason for Permit*. It seemed kind of odd to wait until this point in the application process to ask that question. About 20 minutes later, I reached the counter. I handed in my temporary permit, the form requesting a permanent permit, my birth certificate, and the $70 fee. They took my picture, and, in a few minutes, I walked out with my Permit to Carry Pistols and Revolvers (Connecticut State Pistol Permit). It only took eight weeks and a little over $300. The permit is good for five years.

My experience in obtaining a Connecticut State Pistol Permit illustrates the difference between federal and state gun control laws. Although some may disagree, it is my opinion that federal gun control is not very restrictive. The only federal law that affects the vast majority of firearm purchasers and users is the Brady Act, which requires background checks when guns are purchased through an FFL dealer. Federal law does not require background checks if the firearm is purchased from a private party. In addition, private parties are not required to maintain any type of paperwork on firearm transactions.

Outside of background checks for purchases conducted through an FFL dealer, there are no federal restrictions on gun ownership or possession. There are no federal restrictions on the quantity of guns and ammunition that you can purchase. You can buy as many guns and as much ammunition as you want at any given time. Outside of automatic weapons and other very dangerous firearms regulated through the National Firearms Act (NFA) of 1934, there are no types of firearms that are banned or regulated by the federal government; the federal assault weapons ban expired in 2004. There are no federal laws restricting or regulating either the concealed or open carry of firearms. Finally, outside of NFA weapons (machine guns, etc.), there is no federal registration of firearms. Hence, although various gun rights groups claim that the federal government is always trying to take away your guns or that the restrictions that the federal government imposes on gun owners are too onerous, I would have to disagree. About the only restriction the federal government puts on gun buyers is to submit to a background check if they buy a gun through an FFL dealer. Most background checks take only a few minutes. In my opinion, this is not much of a restriction.

State gun control laws, however, are a different story. Based on my own experience and on a review of state-level statutes, some states, such as Connecticut, have very restrictive gun control laws. In looking at state gun control laws, California is the most restrictive in the nation. California has an assault weapons ban; it requires background checks and a waiting period for all firearm purchases; it restricts multiple gun purchases, concealed carry is may issue; open carry is prohibited; it has a child access prevention (CAP) law; and it has a permit-to-purchase law. New York is next in terms of restrictiveness in that it has all of the gun control laws that California has except a CAP law. Connecticut, Hawaii, and Massachusetts have all of the laws noted above, including a CAP law, except that they allow open carry with a permit. Maryland and New Jersey round out the list of states with the most restrictive gun control laws.

It is important to note, however, that even in these restrictive gun control states, a person can still own and use guns. I was able to obtain a pistol permit in less than two months. This permit allows me to buy almost any gun that I want (except for NFA weapons and most types of assault weapons). I can buy as many guns as I want and as much ammunition as I want. Even with all of the gun control laws that exist in Connecticut, I was still able to get a permit in a relatively short period of time, and my permit is good for five years. So, unless I needed a gun very quickly, or I wanted a very specific type of assault rifle, the laws that currently exist in Connecticut do not overly restrict my ability to buy and possess a gun.

Some may say that it was unreasonable that I had to wait two months to get a permit or that the permit fees were too expensive. I agree that the cost of obtaining the permit was rather exorbitant, but, from what I understand, I will not have to go through this process again and that when I renew my permit in five years, it will only cost me $70. I also agree that two months was a little long to wait, especially given that the state just had to perform a background check, which should have taken less than a day. The local police department actually made it more difficult to obtain my permit than it should have been. I was required by the town police to submit three letters of reference in order to obtain my temporary permit even though the state imposes no such requirement. The police never contacted any of my references, hence calling into question the purpose for this requirement. In addition, the police only allowed pistol permit applicants to get fingerprinted and to submit their applications on Sundays between the hours of 9 and 11 in the morning. I think that it would have been easier for everyone, including the police, if they would have accepted them during normal business hours. Hence, in my opinion, the most restrictive gun control laws are at the state and local levels rather than at the federal level. In addition, some municipalities impose restrictions on gun owners above and beyond those that are mandated by the state.

Another issue is the difference in gun control laws across states and the inability of a private person to transport weapons across state lines. Although there is no federal law prohibiting the transportation of firearms across state lines, several states prohibit or severely restrict such transfers. At the federal level, the Firearm Owners' Protection Act allows persons to transport firearms across state lines, just as long as the person is legally allowed to possess and transport the firearm in both the initial location and the final destination. However, at the state level, some states require persons possessing firearms to have special permits or registrations. California, Hawaii, Massachusetts, New Jersey, and New York have the most restrictions on the interstate transfer of firearms. The easiest way to transport firearms from one place to another is to ship them to yourself. It must be noted, however, that the U.S. Postal Service does not ship handguns. In addition, although a nonresident can buy ammunition in most states, there are some states that allow only residents or permit holders to purchase ammunition. Finally, individuals are only allowed to buy guns in their state of residence from FFL dealers. These various restrictions create frustrations for gun owners, especially for those gun owners passing through states that have permit-to-purchase laws or very restrictive carry laws.

Regarding the effectiveness of gun control measures, most of the research on gun control has found mixed results. Research has found that assault weapons bans do not work. Background checks probably work and may help to reduce firearm-related crime. Restrictive concealed carry laws have no significant effects on crime; they do not cause crime to increase, but they also do not result in a reduction in crime. Regarding permit-to-purchase laws, it appears as if existing research suggests that permits to purchase, which are nothing more than universal background checks, may be effective in reducing gun-related murders. It is important to note that permits to purchase are not licenses required to own or possess a firearm. They are required only for the purchase of firearms. The research on the effects of OCW on crime is minimal and thus inconclusive. Finally, minimum age and CAP laws may reduce accidental firearm deaths and suicides, but the results are mixed. Hence, background checks, permits to purchase, minimum age requirements, and CAP laws have all been found in at least some of the research to reduce firearm-related deaths. Assault weapons bans, carry laws, and other gun control measures either have not been extensively studied or have been found to have no statistically significant effects on firearm-related deaths.

One of the main reasons why many gun control laws are found to be insignificant in the research is that we do not have good data on either guns or crime. The data on the supply of guns in civilian hands are virtually nonexistent. There are some survey data, but they are incomplete and provide no basis for obtaining an estimate of total gun ownership. What is needed are solid data on gun ownership. We need to know how many guns exist and, what types of guns exist. We do not need to know who owns the guns, but at the county, or state level, more complete data on guns levels would be a significant step forward.

Without accurate gun ownership data, it is very difficult to conduct research on the effects of gun control laws on crime. The reason for this is because the only way gun control can affect criminal activity is if gun control affects the supply of guns and if guns have an impact on crime. If gun control does not affect the supply or prevalence of firearms, then gun control cannot affect firearm-related crime in any way whatsoever. In addition, if gun prevalence has no effect on crime, then, gun control cannot affect firearm-related crime. The only way gun control can reduce firearm-related crime is if gun control reduces the supply of firearms and if firearm prevalence increases firearm-related criminal activity.

Regarding crime data, we need to know in more detail and with more completeness how often guns are used in the commission of crimes. We need to know what types of guns are used (handguns versus long guns). I am unsure why law enforcement agencies do not track these type of data, but they are necessary in order to determine if firearm-related crime, and especially murder, is more or less prevalent in areas with above-average gun ownership levels.

We also need much better data on self-protective behaviors. We need to know if a person engaged in self-defense during the commission of a crime, if a firearm was used, and, if so, what type of firearm was used. We need to know how many people in a given year engage in self-protective behaviors at both the state and county level. We need to know the outcome of these self-protective behaviors. Did the victim escape? Was the victim hurt? Did the perpetrator run away? We do not have answers to these questions with the current data. We only have survey data, and their reliability and objectivity have been questioned by many. It would be best if police reported these data, but, to my knowledge, these data are either not reported or are not publicly available.

Unfortunately, some of the above data may be difficult to obtain. The police may be constrained by limited resources and may not be able to report the needed crime data, especially data on firearms. Also, data on gun ownership may be difficult to obtain given privacy issues and Second Amendment concerns. One way to obtain data on gun ownership would be to use existing surveys or censuses more effectively. For example, questions on gun ownership and self-protective behaviors can be added to the U.S. Census, the American Community Survey, and the General Social Surveys. These surveys are well-known and well respected. Data obtained from these surveys can be used to better determine the effectiveness of gun control measures and the impact of gun availability on crime.

Of course, the primary reason many people think we need gun control is that they believe that we have a lot of crime and firearm violence in the United States. If crime was not a problem, then there would be little need to discuss the merits of gun control. But is crime really as bad as we think it is? The answer is no. The murder rate is at its lowest level since 1960. The murder rate in 1960 was 5.1 (per 100,000 persons). In 1980, the murder rate was 10.2. In 2012, the murder rate was 4.7. Rape, robbery, and aggravated assault are also at their lowest levels in 40 years. The only type of crime that is up is mass shooting, and, although mass shootings are very tragic and horrific, they are also very rare. Hence, even though the number of mass shootings per year is up, very few people in a given year are killed in a mass shooting. Therefore, according to the available crime data, there is less need for gun control now than there was 50 years ago. Likewise, given these very low crime rates, there is also less need for citizens to arm themselves now than there was 50 years ago.

It is important to note, however, that the firearm suicide rate is up since 1999, but the firearm accidental death rate has declined during the same period. The increase in the suicide rate is important, because many more people die from firearm suicides than they do from firearm homicides. Relatively few people die from firearm accidents.

The next important question is "do armed citizens actually help lower the crime rate?" The available data suggest that very few crime victims actually defend themselves with a gun. In fact, according to the National Crime Victimization Survey, only 0.4% of persons involved in a criminal incident defend themselves with a gun. One of the reasons put forth by gun rights activists for unfettered gun ownership is that private citizens need the ability to defend themselves against criminal attacks. However, given that crime rates are at their lowest levels in decades, and given that very few victims engage in self-protective behaviors involving a firearm, then why do citizens need guns to defend themselves?

So what should be done to reduce gun violence? Any proposal should be based on the current research on the effectiveness of gun control measures. If a measure is effective in reducing firearm-related deaths, then it should be considered for adoption. In addition to the effectiveness of the measures, any proposal should take into consideration the costs associated with obtaining any necessary permits and the uniformity of gun control across the United States. It cost over $300 for me to obtain my pistol permit in Connecticut; that is rather excessive, especially for a lower-income person. Also, there are issues with differing gun control measures across the United States. Gun owners sometimes find it difficult to travel between states and to purchase guns and ammunition in states other than their own. These inconsistencies in the laws create needles frustrations for gun owners and put them in legal peril if they run afoul of the varying state laws. Any proposed gun control system should be uniform across the United States. Finally, it is important to remember that gun control is only one of the many factors that affect the overall level of firearm-related deaths in the United States. There are many other factors (economic, social, health) that affect firearm deaths, and any proposed system should address these other issues as well. Otherwise, the overall level of gun violence will not be significantly reduced. In fact, in most of the research on gun control, economic and social factors have much larger effects on gun deaths than gun control does.

I propose that there should be a national permit-to-purchase program. The permit would be recognized nationwide and would require a criminal and mental health background check, a firearm safety course, and some time on a firing range. The minimum age requirement for this permit would be 18. Permit holders would be al to securely transport their firearms anywhere in the United States. Additional training and background checks would be required for OCW and CCW and for the purchase of assault weapons.

Finally, FFL dealer paperwork should be reduced. Instead of having indefinitely maintain the records of all firearm transactions, FFL dealers should only have to notify authorities (FBI or state law enforcement agencies) if they buy or sell a handgun or an assault (semiautomatic) rifle. The reason for this is that these types of weapons are the ones used most frequently in gun-related murders and mass shooting. Dealers would not have to notify authorities if they buy or sell a shotgun or a nonsemiautomatic rifle. In addition, the dealer would not have to maintain records on any firearm transaction.

The background check requirements and prohibitions would be similar to those currently in affect at the federal level. Permits would be valid for at least one year, and there would be periodic checks by the issuing authority in order to ensure that the permit holder is still legally allowed to possess a firearm. Under this proposed system, every effort would be made to encourage states to provide timely and complete information to the background check system regarding criminal activities and mental health histories. If states do not provide timely information, then even the most well-thought-out plan will fail.

Although this system may seem onerous, it would greatly simplify gun ownership in the United States. One reason would be that the permits would be recognized nationwide. A permit holder would be able to buy a gun anywhere in the United States. Gun owners would not live in fear of violating state or local laws regarding gun ownership, gun possession, or the transportation of firearm across state line. Also, local and state authorities would not be allowed to impose additional requirements on gun owners.

My proposed system is designed to bring simplicity to gun buying and owning. The biggest problem and frustration with the current system is that it is just too confusing. There are too many overlapping and inconsistent rules and regulations concerning firearms. Take, for example, my experience with obtaining a pistol permit in Connecticut. Although the state devised the rules and requirements regarding pistol permits, my town imposed additional burdens, most of which I contend did nothing to enhance public safety but only resulted in frustration among gun owners and gave further credence to the belief that the *government is trying to take away our guns*. In what way did making me show up on a Sunday morning to hand in my permit application reduce gun violence? I am pretty sure it did not.

Would criminals apply for firearm permits? Probably not. There are more than enough guns in circulation to keep the criminal element supplied for years to come. Then why bother with a national permit system? Because research has shown that of all of the existing gun control measures, background checks are one of the most effective measures in reducing firearm violence. Hence, the proposed system would act like a universal background check system with consistent rules nationwide. It would provide protection to gun owners while at the same time providing law enforcement agencies with better tools to combat firearm-related crimes. Is it perfect? No. But at least it is an evidence-based gun control measure that may reduce firearm violence.

Finally, the goal of gun control should be to reduce crime, particularly firearm-related crime. Unfortunately, given the current state of crime and gun data, it is difficult to determine if any gun control measure is truly effective in this regard. Better data would allow us to ascertain the effectiveness of any and all gun control measure and could put to rest once and for all the question of whether more guns mean more crime.

References

Anglemyer, Andrew, Tara Horvath, and George Rutherford. 2014. The accessibility of firearms and risk for suicide and homicide victimization among household members. *Annals of Internal Medicine*, 160, 101–110.

Ayers, Ian and John Donohue. 2003. Shooting down the more guns, less crime hypothesis. *Stanford Law Review*, 55, 1193–1314.

Bartley, William and Mark Cohen. 1998. The effect of concealed weapons laws: An extreme bound analysis. *Economic Inquiry*, 36, 258–265.

Benson, Bruce and Brent Mast. 2001. Privately produced general deterrence. *Journal of Law and Economics*, 44, S2, 725–746.

Bjelopera, Jerome, Erin Bagalman, Sarah Caldwell, Kristin Finklea, and Gail McCallion. 2013. Public mass shootings in the United States: Selected implications for federal public health and safety policy. Congressional Research Service report: Washington, DC.

Black, Dan and Daniel Nagin. 1998. Do right-to-carry laws deter violent crime? *The Journal of Legal Studies*, 27, 209–219.

Brauer, Jurgen. 2013. The US firearms industry: Produciton and supply. *Small Arms Survey*: Geneva, Switzerland.

Bronars, Stephen and John Lott. 1998. Criminal deterrence, geographic spillovers, and the right to carry concealed handguns. *The American Economic Review*, 88, 2, 475–479.

Bugg, David and Philip Yang. 2004. Trends in women's gun ownership, 1973–2002. *International Journal of Comparative and Applied Criminal Justice*, 28, 2, 169–188.

Cao, Liquin, Francis Cullen, and Bruce Link. 1997. The social determinants of gun ownership: Self-protection in an urban environment. *Criminology*, 35, 4, 629–657.

CDC. Various years. Fatal Injury Reports. Washington, DC: Centers for Disease Control and Prevention, National Center for Injury Prevention and Control.

Chamlin, Mitchell. 2014. An assessment of the intended and unintended consequences of Arizona's Self-Defense, Home Protection Act. *Journal of Crime and Justice*, 37, 3, 327–338.

Chapman, Simon, Philip Alpers, Kim Agho, and Mairwen Jones. 2006. Australia's 1996 gun law reforms: Faster falls in firearm deaths, firearm suicides, and a decade without mass shootings. *Injury Prevention*, 12, 365–372.

Cheng, Cheng and Mark Hoekstra. 2012. Does strengthening self-defense law deter crime or escalate violence? Evidence from expansions to castle doctrine. *Journal of Human Resources*, 48, 3, 821–854.

Conner, Kenneth and Yueying Zhong. 2003. State firearm laws and the rates of suicide in men and women. *American Journal of Preventive Medicine*, 25, 320–324.

Cook, Phillip and Jens Ludwig. 1997. Guns in America: National survey on private
ownership and use of firearms. National Institute of Justice, NCJ 165476.

Crifasi, Cassandra, John Meyers, Jon Vernick, and Daniel Webster. 2015. Effects of
changes in permit-to-purchase handgun laws in Connecticut and Missouri
on suicide rates. *Preventive Medicine*, 79, 43–49.

Dezhbakhsh, Hashem and Paul Rubin. 1998. Lives saved or lives lost? The effects
of concealed handgun laws on crime. *The American Economic Review*, 88, 2,
468–474.

Donohue, John. 2003. The impact of concealed-carry laws. In *Evaluating Gun
Policy: Effects on Crime and Violence*, John Ludwig and Philip Cook, eds.,
The Brookings Institution: Washington, DC, 287–341.

Duggan, Mark. 2001. More guns, more crime. *The Journal of Political Economy*, 5,
109, 1086–1114.

Duggan, Mark. 2003. Gun and suicide. In *Evaluating Gun Policy: Effects on Crime
and Violence*, John Ludwig and Phillip Cook, eds., The Brookings Institution:
Washington, DC, 41–73.

Duwe, Grant, Tomislav Kovandzic, and Carlisle Moody. 2002. The impact of right-
to-carry concealed firearm laws on public mass shootings. *Homicide Studies*,
6, 4, 271–296.

Federal Bureau of Investigation. Various years. Crime in the United States.

Fisher, Marc and Dan Eggen. 2012. "Stand your ground" laws coincide with jump
in justifiable homicide cases. *Washington Post*, April 7.

Fleegler, Eric, Lois Lee, Michael Monuteaux, David Hemenway, and Rebekah
Mannix. 2013. Firearm legislation and firearm-related fatalities in the United
States. *JAMA Internal Medicine*, 173, 9, 732–740.

Follman, Mark, Gavin Aronsen, and Deanna Pan. 2016. A guide to mass shootings in America. *Mother Jones*. Available at http://www.motherjones.com
/politics/2012/12/mass-shootings-mother-jones-full-data.

Gius, Mark. 2008. Measuring the effect of gun control laws on gun ownership
using the Behavioral Risk Factor Surveillance System. *Journal of Business and
Economic Perspectives*, 34, 1, 48–57.

Gius, Mark. 2009. The effect of gun ownership rates on homicide rates: A state-
level analysis. *Applied Economics Letters*, 16, 1687–1690.

Gius, Mark. 2011. The effects of gun ownership rates and gun control laws on suicide rates. *New York Economic Review*, 42, 35–46.

Gius, Mark. 2014. An examination of the effects of concealed weapons laws and
assault weapons bans on state-level murder rates. *Applied Economics Letters*,
21, 4, 265–267.

Gius, Mark. 2015a. The impact of state and federal assault weapons bans on public
mass shooting. *Applied Economics Letters*, 22, 4, 281–284.

Gius, Mark. 2015b. The impact of minimum age and child access prevention laws
on firearm-related youth suicides and unintentional deaths. *The Social Science
Journal*, 52, 168–175.

Gius, Mark. 2015c. The effects of state and federal background checks on state-
level gun-related murder rates. *Applied Economics*, 47, 38, 4090–4101.

Gius, Mark. 2016. The relationship between stand-your-ground laws and crime: A
state-level analysis. *Social Science Journal*.

Helland, Eric and Alexander Tabarrok. 2004. Using placebo laws to test "more guns, less crime." *Advances in Economic Analysis & Policy*, 4, 1, 1–7.

Huff-Corzine, Lin, James McCutcheon, Jay Corzine, John Jarvis, Melissa Tetzlaff-Bemiller, Mindy Weller, and Matt Landon. 2013. Shooting for accuracy: Comparing data sources on mass murder. *Homicide Studies*, 18, 1, 105–124.

Irvin, Nathan, Karin Rhodes, Rose Cheney, and Douglas Wiebe. 2014. Evaluating the effect of state regulation of federally licensed firearm dealers on firearm homicide. *American Journal of Public Health*, 104, 8, 1384–1386.

Jonsson, Patrik. 2013. Racial bias and "stand your ground" laws: What the data show. *The Christian Science Monitor*, August 6.

Kalesan, Bindu, Marcos Villareal, Katherine Keyes, and Sandro Galea. 2016. Gun ownership and social gun culture. *Injury Prevention*, 22, 3, 216–220.

Kleck, Gary and Marc Gertz. 1995. Armed resistance to crime: The prevalence and nature of self-defense with a gun. *Journal of Criminal Law and Criminology*, 86, 1, 150–187.

Kleck, Gary and Michael Hogan. 1999. National case-control study of homicide offending and gun ownership. *Social Problems*, 46, 2, 275–293.

Kleck, Gary and E. Britt Patterson. 1993. The impact of gun control and gun ownership levels on violence rates. *Journal of Quantitative Criminology*, 9, 3, 249–287.

Koper, Christopher. 2004. An updated assessment of the Federal Assault Weapons Ban: Impacts on gun markets and gun violence, 1994–2003. Report to the National Institute of Justice, US Department of Justice.

Koper, Christopher and Jeffrey Roth. 2001. The impact of the 1994 Federal Assault Weapon Ban on gun violence outcomes: An assessment of multiple outcome measures and some lessons for policy evaluation. *Journal of Quantitative Criminology*, 17, 1, 33–74.

Kovandzic, Tomislav and Thomas Marvell. 2003. Right-to-carry concealed handguns and violent crime: Crime control through gun decontrol? *Criminology and Public Policy*, 2, 3, 363–396.

Kovandzic, Tomislav, Thomas Marvell, and Lynne Vieraitis. 2005. The impact of "shall-issue" concealed handgun laws on violent crime rates: Evidence from panel data for large urban cities. *Homicide Studies*, 9, 4, 292–323.

Lang, Matthew. 2013. Firearm background checks and suicide. *The Economic Journal*, 123, 1085–1099.

Leenaars, Antoon and David Lester. 1997. The effects of gun control on the unintentional death rate from firearms in Canada. *Journal of Safety Research*, 28, 3, 119–122.

Lester, David. 1988. Gun control, gun ownership, and suicide prevention. *Suicide and Life-Threatening Behavior*, 18, 176–180.

Lester, David. 1993. Firearm availability and unintentional deaths from firearms. *Journal of Safety Research*, 24, 3, 167–169.

Lester, David and Mary Murrell. 1981. The influence of gun control laws on the incidence of accidents with guns: A preliminary study. *Accident Analysis and Prevention*, 13, 4, 357–359.

Lester, David and Mary Murrell. 1982. The preventive effect of strict gun control laws on suicide and homicide. *Suicide and Life-Threatening Behavior*, 12, 131–140.

Lott, John. 1998. The concealed-handgun debate. *The Journal of Legal Studies*, 27, 1, 221–243.

Lott, John and William Landes. 2000. Multiple victim public shootings. Unpublished paper.

Lott, John and David Mustard. 1997. Crime, deterrence, and right-to-carry concealed handguns. *The Journal of Legal Studies*, 26, 1, 1–68.

Lott, John and John Whitley. 2001. Safe-storage gun laws: Accidental deaths, suicides, and crime. *Journal of Law and Economics*, 44, S2, 659–689.

Ludwig, Jens. 1998. Concealed-gun-carrying laws and violent crime: Evidence from state panel data. *International Review of Law and Economics*, 18, 3, 239–254.

Ludwig, Jens and Philip Cook. 2000. Homicide and suicide rates associated with implementation of the Brady Handgun Violence Prevention Act. *JAMA*, 284, 585–591.

Maltz, Michael and Joseph Targonski. 2002. A note on the use of county-level UCR data. *Journal of Quantitative Criminology*, 18, 3, 297–318.

Marvell, Thomas. 2001. The impact of banning juvenile gun possession. *Journal of Law and Economics*, 44, S2, 691–713.

McClellan, Chandler and Erdal Tekin. 2012. Stand your ground laws, homicides, and injuries. NBER working paper 18187.

Miller, Matthew, Deborah Azrael, and David Hemenway. 2002. Rates of household firearm ownership and homicide across US regions and states, 1988–1997. *American Journal of Public Health*, 92, 12, 1988–1993.

Miller, Matthew, Deborah Azrael, David Hemenway, and Simon Lippmann. 2006. The association between changes in household firearm ownership and rates of suicide in the United States, 1981–2002. *Injury Prevention*, 12, 178–182.

Monuteaux, Michael, Lois Lee, David Hemenway, Rebekah Mannix, and Eric Fleegler. 2015. Firearm ownership and violent crime in the US. *American Journal of Preventive Medicine*, 49, 2, 207–214.

Moody, Carlisle. 2001. Testing for the effects of concealed weapons laws: Specification errors and robustness. *Journal of Law and Economics*, 44, S2, 799–813.

Moody, Carlisle and Thomas Marvell. 2005. Guns and crime. *Southern Economic Journal*, 71, 4, 720–736.

Olson, David and Michael Maltz. 2001. Right-to-carry concealed weapon laws and homicide in large US counties: The effect on weapon types, victim characteristics, and victim–offender relationships. *Journal of Law and Economics*, 44, S2, 747–770.

Plant, Michael and Jennifer Truman. 2013. Firearm violence, 1993–2011. US Department of Justice, Bureau of Justice Statistics, May.

Plassman, Florenz and T. Nicolaus Tideman. 2001. Does the right to carry concealed handguns deter countable crimes? Only a count analysis can say. *Journal of Law and Economics*, 44, 2, 771–798.

Ren, Ling, Yan Zhang, and Jihong Solomon Zhao. 2012. The deterrent effect of the castle doctrine law on burglary in Texas: A tale of outcomes in Houston and Dallas. *Crime & Delinquency*, 61, 8, 1127–1151.

Ross, Catherine. 2001. Neighborhoods and guns in middle America. *Sociological Focus*, 34, 3, 287–298.

Rubin, Paul and Hashem Dezhbakhsh. 2003. The effect of concealed handgun laws on crime: Beyond the dummy variables. *International Review of Law and Economics*, 23, 199–216.

Ruddell, Rick and G. Larry Mays. 2005. State background checks and firearm homicides. *Journal of Criminal Justice*, 33, 127–136.

Rudolph, Kara, Elizabeth Stuart, Jon Vernick, and Daniel Webster. 2015. Association between Connecticut's permit-to-purchase handgun law and homicides. *American Journal of Public Health*, 105, 8, e49–e54.

1967. *Sacramento Bee*, A1–A10.

Sen, Bisakha and Anantachai Panjamapirom. 2012. State background checks for gun purchase and firearm deaths: An exploratory analysis. *Preventive Medicine*, 55, 346–350.

Siegel, Michael, Craig Ross, and Charles King. 2013. The relationship between gun ownership and firearm homicide rates in the United States, 1981–2010. *American Journal of Public Health*, 11, 103, 2098–2105.

Siegel, Michael, Craig Ross, and Charles King. 2014a. Examining the relationship between the prevalence of guns and homicide rates in the USA using a new and improved state-level gun ownership proxy. *Injury Prevention*, 20, 424–426.

Siegel, Michael, Yamrot Negussie, Sarah Vanture, Jane Pleskunas, Craig Ross, and Charles King. 2014b. The relationship between gun ownership and stranger and nonstranger firearm homicide rates in the United States, 1981–2010. *American Journal of Public Health*, 104, 10, 1912–1919.

2007. *Small Arms Survey*. Cambridge, MA: Cambridge, University Press.

Sommers, Paul. 1984. The effect of gun control laws on suicide rates. *Atlantic Economic Journal*, 12, 67–69.

Sumner, Steven, Peter Layde, and Clare Guse. 2008. Firearm death rates and association with level of firearm purchase background check. *American Journal of Preventive Medicine*, 35, 1, 1–6.

Webster, Daniel, Jon Vernick, Emma McGinty, and Ted Alcorn. 2013. Preventing the diversion of guns through effective firearm sales laws. In *Reducing Gun Violence in America: Informing Policy with Evidence and Analysis*, Daniel Webster and Jon Vernick, eds., The Johns Hopkins University Press: Baltimore, 109–121.

Webster, Daniel, Cassandra Kercher Crifasi, and Jon Vernick. 2014. Effects of the repeal of Missouri's handgun purchaser licensing law on homicides. *Journal of Urban Health*, 91, 2, 293–302.

Wintemute, Garen. 2015a. Alcohol misuse, firearm violence perpetration, and public policy in the United States. *Preventive Medicine*, 79, 15–21.

Wintemute, Garen. 2015b. The epidemiology of firearm violence in the twenty-first century United States. *Annual Review of Public Health*, 36, 5–19.

Yang, Bijou and David Lester. 1991. The effect of gun availability on suicide rates. *Atlantic Economic Journal*, 19, 74.

Zeoli, April, Rebecca Malinski, and Brandon Turchan. 2016. Risks and targeted interventions: Firearms in intimate partner violence. *Epidemiologic Reviews*, 38, 125–139.

Index